617.47

Skeleton

This book is due for return on or before the last

a X-rays

Also in this series:

Self-assessment in Limb X-ray Interpretation
ISBN: 978-1-905539-13-0 · 2006
Self-assessment in Paediatric Musculoskeletal Trauma X-rays
ISBN: 978-1-905539-34-5 · 2008

Forthcoming:

Self-assessment in Musculoskeletal Pathology

Other health and social care books from M&K include

Routine Blood Results Explained 2/e
ISBN: 978-1-905539-38-3 · 2008
A Guide to Research for Podiatrists
ISBN: 978-1-905539-41-3 · 2007
The ECG Workbook
ISBN: 978-1-905539-14-7 · 2008
Arterial Blood Gas Analysis: An easy learning guide
ISBN: 978-1-905539-04-8 · 2008
Haemodynamic Monitoring & Manipulation: An easy learning guide
ISBN: 978-1-905539-46-8 · 2009
The Management of COPD in Primary and Secondary Care
ISBN: 978-1-905539-28-4 · 2007
The Clinician's Guide to Chronic Disease Management for
Long Term Conditions: A cognitive–behavioural approach
ISBN: 978-1-905539-15-4 · 2008

Self Assessment in

Axial Skeleton Musculoskeletal Trauma X-rays

Karen Sakthivel-Wainford

H.D.C.R (R), PGCert, MSc
Advanced Radiographer Practitioner, Leeds General Infirmary, UK

Self-assessment in Axial Skeleton Musculoskeletal Trauma X-rays
Karen Sakthivel-Wainford

ISBN: 978-1-905539-47-5

First published 2009

British Library Cataloguing in Publication Data
A catalogue record for this book is available from the British Library

Notice
Clinical practice and medical knowledge constantly evolve. Standard safety precautions must be followed, but, as knowledge is broadened by research, changes in practice, treatment and drug therapy may become necessary or appropriate. Readers must check the most current product information provided by the manufacturer of each drug to be administered and verify the dosages and correct administration, as well as contraindications. It is the responsibility of the practitioner, utilising the experience and knowledge of the patient, to determine dosages and the best treatment for each individual patient. Any brands mentioned in this book are as examples only and are not endorsed by the Publisher. Neither the publisher nor the authors assume any liability for any injury and/or damage to persons or property arising from this publication.

The Publisher
To contact M&K Publishing write to:
M&K Update Ltd · The Old Bakery · St. John's Street
Keswick · Cumbria CA12 5AS
Tel: 01768 773030 · Fax: 01768 781099
publishing@mkupdate.co.uk
www.mkupdate.co.uk

Designed and typeset in Usherwood Book by Mary Blood
Printed in England by Reeds Printers, Penrith.

Contents

Acknowledgements

To the Radiology departments of Leeds General Infirmary, and Wharfedale General Hospital, for their continued support and the use of radiographs in this book.

To Katy Johnson for participating in this book.

To Fiona Carmichael, for help and support when I have to lecture on mandible and facial trauma.

In memory of my beloved mother, Marjorie Wainford, who has not long left this world. Her courage and strength of mind through difficulties will always be an inspiration to me.

Introduction

Many radiographer practitioners are now continuing to expand their reporting skills from the appendicular skeleton to include the axial skeleton in trauma. Other allied professions may also be reviewing axial skeleton trauma radiographs, for instance nurse practitioners (particularly in cases of hip trauma, in our trust), physiotherapists, etc., and hence wish to increase their knowledge. This book, like the others in the series is written specifically for radiographers, be they 'red dotting' radiographers, commenting radiographers, radiographer practitioners or nurse practitioners.

Many radiographers initially fear reviewing axial skeleton radiographs, understandably, as missing an injury may have dire consequences. But with training, audit and care this fear can be overcome; and one can look forward to the challenge of axial radiograph reporting.

The book is intended to be like sitting in on a reporting session with a radiologist or radiographer practitioner, where you are asked to report/comment on the radiograph, but also asked some questions and given feedback. It is intended to support whatever course you have done, whether it be reporting, 'red dotting' or commenting, or to encourage you to go on 'that course'. It can be a revision book, or help in preparation for an assessment. However you use it, I hope it will encourage you to read more and research more into musculoskeletal trauma.

As axial trauma radiographs can be difficult to review, the book starts with several chapters, to introduce or revise specific axial trauma. The first chapter discusses mechanisms of injury of major trauma and is written by Katy Johnson, a Radiographer Practitioner working at Leeds General Infirmary. This is followed by a chapter on pelvic trauma. The next chapter looks at reviewing cervical spine trauma radiographs.

Then a series of trauma cases of the axial skeleton is presented, on which you are asked to write reports, and sometimes answer a few questions (the answers are over the page). This section is divided into six chapters: trauma cases of the pelvis; of the hip and femur; the cervical spine; dorsal and lumbar spine; the skull, facial bones and mandible (15 cases in each chapter); the last chapter being 25 mixed cases. It is preferable to work your way through the book from start to finish. However, if you feel you need revision on, say, cervical spine radiographs, then you can flick to the chapter on reviewing the cervical spine and then to the cases on the cervical spine.

Each case has appropriate clinical history, although this may not be the original history in order to anonymise the case. Some of the cases may not have side markers; these may have been removed whilst removing patients' details.

Note: Specific references appear at the end of Chapter 1. There is also a general reading list/bibliography on page 267.

1.

Mechanisms of injury

Katy Johnson

In order to understand how injuries occur, we must recognise the importance of the mechanism of injury in determining injury patterns. Each situation will be different, but by obtaining an accurate assessment of how the accident happened and the mechanisms involved, certain injury patterns can be predicted. This chapter looks at some basic laws of physics and explains how these relate to the trauma setting.

There are several mechanisms which are highly predictive of serious injury due to the forces involved (Greaves, Porter and Ryan, 2001):

- Fall of more than 6 metres
- Pedestrian or cyclist hit by car
- Death of other occupant in same vehicle
- Ejection from vehicle/bike
- Major vehicular deformity or significant intrusion into passenger space
- Extrication time more than 20 minutes
- Vehicular roll-over
- Penetrating injury to head or torso
- All shotgun wounds.

All of the above mechanisms share the same common factor – they arise as a direct result of significant energy transfer. But before we can appreciate how the injuries occur, we need to understand some basic laws of motion.

Basic laws of motion

Many injuries occur as a result of the transfer of **Kinetic Energy** (KE) – this is the energy of motion and can be defined as:

$KE = \frac{1}{2}mv^2$

where m = mass and v = velocity.

Newton's First Law states that an object which is at rest will stay at rest and an object which is in motion will stay in motion in a straight line unless acted upon by an external force. This is often referred to as the law of inertia.

Newton's Second Law builds on the first and states that force (F) is equal to the product of mass (m) and acceleration (a):

F = ma

which means that force is associated with a change in momentum, i.e. acceleration or deceleration.

Newton's Third Law states that for every action, there is an equal and opposite reaction.

This in turn brings in another basic law of motion, that energy cannot be created or destroyed, but it can change in form or be absorbed. It is this energy change and absorption that affects the human body and produces a specific pattern of injuries.

Once we understand these laws, we can relate them to the effects they have upon the human body in real life trauma situations.

Impact characteristics

Mechanical injuries are produced when two bodies collide and the kinetic energy is dissipated. There are several characteristics of the collision which influence the degree of injury to the human body (Nowak and Handford, 1999).

The total **amount of energy** which is transferred from one object to another plays a massive role in the damage sustained. The heavier an object is and the faster it is moving, the more kinetic energy it possesses. If you double the mass of an object, you double the kinetic energy, whereas if you double the velocity of it, four times the kinetic energy is created. Therefore, if a person who has a mass of 70kg drives his car with a velocity of 30km/hour, he will have a kinetic energy of 31500 J – 70 x (30 x 30)/2. If that same person travels just 10km/hour faster, he will have a kinetic energy of 56000 J – 70 x (40 x 40)/2. If he then crashes his car into a tree, the car stops and the body carries on moving until an external force, such as the steering wheel, stops it (law of inertia). The internal organs then carry on moving until they are stopped, for example, by the ribcage, and subsequent injuries arise from this.

The amount of time over which the energy is imparted also affects the severity of the injury. The longer the **duration of the impact**, the more the body tissues can absorb and spread the impact, whereas a much shorter duration is more likely to result in extensive damage. For example, a bullet imparts massive physical injury as it is travelling at extremely high velocity and therefore has a very short duration of impact. Compare this to someone being stabbed with a knife – although still a significant mechanism of injury, the velocity of the knife is much less than the bullet, and the force is thus significantly less.

The **surface area** which is affected also plays a large part in the severity of injury. The larger the impact area, the more tissues there are to absorb and dissipate the kinetic energy. When a motorcyclist wears a helmet, he is creating a wider impact zone, so that in the event of an accident, the energy is spread around the helmet rather than into the skull and brain.

The **characteristics of the tissues** which are affected by the impact are also directly related to the injuries sustained. Tissues which have more flexibility and elasticity can withstand greater impact than fixed and rigid structures, such as bone. In a high-speed road traffic accident, aortic rupture is the most common cause of sudden death. The descending aorta is relatively fixed in position but the aortic arch is unsupported. Therefore, a sudden deceleration can cause the aortic arch to shear off from the descending aorta, resulting in an injury which is usually fatal within seconds (Greaves, Porter and Ryan, 2001).

The **patient's age** will also significantly affect the pattern and severity of the injuries sustained. The strength of healthy adult bone requires an extremely large amount of kinetic energy to result in significant damage (McConnell, Eyres and Nightingale, 2005). The high collagen levels in children's bones mean that they are much more flexible and elastic than an adult's and then as a person gets older, their bones become much more brittle. However, a child is much more likely to suffer serious injury from a major incident than an adult. Their small size means that an impact is more likely to involve more organs and structures.

Mechanisms

Mechanisms of injury can be broadly divided into:

- blunt
- penetrating
- thermal
- blast.

An incident may be a combination of these, but the common factor is that they all occur as a direct result of energy transfer to the body tissues. For the purposes of this text, where skeletal trauma is the key theme, thermal and blast injuries will not be discussed.

Blunt trauma

By far the most common mechanism of injury, blunt trauma occurs over a large surface area. It is usually sustained through road traffic accidents, falls and assaults with blunt objects. It can be further sub-divided by the forces which are involved:

● direct impact/compression – direct pressure on tissues
● shear – organs and tissues move relative to each other
● rotation – organs and tissues twist relative to each other

although in reality these forces are often found in combination (Greaves, Porter and Ryan, 2001). These different forces produce different patterns of injuries, depending on the incident.

Road traffic accidents

Motor vehicle collisions are the third most common cause of death worldwide, causing more than 1 million deaths and 38 million injuries each year. They can occur in many ways – vehicle versus vehicle, vehicle versus pedestrian, vehicle versus stationary object and motorcycle and cycle injuries. It is important for the A&E clinician to obtain an accurate assessment of the incident scene in order to predict a pattern of injuries. There are many factors they need to know:

● What was the estimated speed of impact?
● What type of collision was it, i.e. frontal, side or rear?
● What was the patient's position within vehicle, i.e. driver, front or rear seat passenger?
● Did the vehicle roll over?
● Were the occupants wearing seatbelts?
● Were they ejected? If so, how far?
● Did the car have airbags that were deployed?
● How long did extrication take?
● What was the type of vehicle and the extent of damage to it?

(Brooks, Mahoney and Hodgetts, 2007)

Falls

Falls account for a high proportion of attendances at A&E and are the leading cause of injury-related death in people over the age of 65. These types of falls are often from a low height, i.e. sitting or standing, but because of the patient's age there are often many other contributing factors and they may result in high morbidity and mortality rates.

Falls from heights usually result in multiple injuries. The patterns of injuries are affected by:

● the height of the fall (and therefore the speed of impact)
● the surface fallen onto
● the position of the body on impact.

People who fall feet first are likely to suffer lower limb fractures such as calcaneal fractures and pilon fractures from direct forces and then as the force is transmitted up through their body, vertical shear fractures through the pelvis and compression fractures of vertebrae. They may also suffer deceleration injuries, such as transection of the aorta.

Penetrating trauma

Penetrating trauma often occurs as a result of an assault by another person, i.e. stabbing with a knife or shooting, but can also occur by impalement by an object which would usually be in combination with blunt trauma. Injuries are usually categorised by the amount of energy transfer involved. Stab wounds are low energy transfer injuries which cause direct tissue damage along a straight track. Severity of injury depends on the size of the blade, how deep the wound is and the location of the wound. Gunshot wounds on the other hand are high energy transfer injuries due to the high velocity of the bullet. They inflict much greater tissue damage due to the increased forces involved and do so in three ways:

- laceration and crushing
- cavitation – a 'permanent' cavity is caused by the path of the bullet itself and a 'temporary' cavity is formed by stretching of the tissues
- shock waves travel ahead and to the sides.

(Brooks, Mahoney and Hodgetts, 2007)

Conclusion

An understanding of the laws of motion and mechanisms involved in producing injuries allows certain patterns of injuries to be predicted and dictates the imaging that needs to be conducted in order to diagnose both the obvious and occult injuries. The radiographer plays as big a part as any in the trauma team in providing the necessary imaging, so that treatment may be sought as quickly as possible, thereby providing a better outcome for the patient.

Katy Johnson is a Reporting Radiographer Practitioner at Leeds General Infirmary – a very large and busy teaching hospital. She has a particular interest in trauma and orthopaedics.

References

Brooks, A., Mahoney, P.F., and Hodgetts, T.J. (2007). *Major Trauma*. Edinburgh: Churchill Livingstone.

Greaves, I., Porter, K.M., and Ryan, J.M. (eds.) (2001). *Trauma Care Manual*. London: Arnold.

McConnell, J., Eyres, R., and Nightingale, J. (2005). *Interpreting Trauma Radiographs*. Oxford: Blackwell Publishing.

Nowak, T.J., and Handford, A.G. (1999). *Essentials of Pathophysiology: Concepts and Applications for the Health Care Professions*, 2nd edn.

2.

Pelvic fractures

Karen Sakthivel-Wainford

The pelvis is a ring-like structure, the major functions of which are weight-bearing support for the spine and protection of the viscera within the pelvic cavity. This ring-like structure consists of three principal bones: the paired innominate bones and the sacrum. Haemorrhage is a serious and frequent complication of pelvic fractures. Also there is a high incidence of associated injuries to the viscera within the pelvic ring. Acute renal failure can be induced by pelvic haemorrhage, pelvic sepsis or both. Hence it is imperative that pelvic fractures are identified speedily, of course with radiographic assistance.

To be able to recognise pelvic trauma on a radiograph, we first need to be able to identify normal pelvic anatomy. The pelvic ring consists of two arches. The main arch extends superiorly and posteriorly from one acetabulum to the other and contains the large wings of the iliac bone and the sacrum. This is the main weight-bearing component of the pelvis and is referred to as the posterior or femorosacral arch. The anterior arch extends from the acetabulum inferiorly and anteriorly to the opposite acetabulum through the pubic bones, and consists of the anterior third of the pelvic ring.

Although these are the main arches, some other texts comment on two further smaller rings, formed by the pubic and ischial bones and forming the obturator foramina.

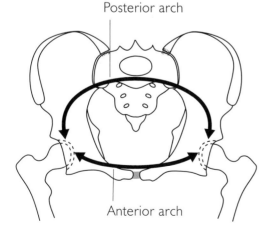

Figure 2.1
Arches of the pelvic ring

Pelvic ligaments

The stability of the pelvis is dependent on the integrity of the ligaments about the sacroiliac joints and those extending from the sacrum across the pelvis to the ischial spine and tuberosity. The main ligaments about the sacroiliac joints, the sacroiliac ligaments, are situated posteriorly (these are the strongest ligaments in the body). Other ligaments of the pelvis are the sacrotuberous ligament, a strong broad band extending from the lateral aspect of the dorsum of the sacrum to the ischial tuberosity and forming a portion of the pelvic outlet. The sacrospinous ligament arises from the lateral aspect of the sacrum and coccyx, anterior to the sacrotuberous ligament, and inserts on the ischial spine. The iliolumbar ligaments attach from the tip of the fifth lumbar transverse process to the iliac crest; and the lateral lumbosacral ligaments spread downward from the fifth transverse process to the sacrum.

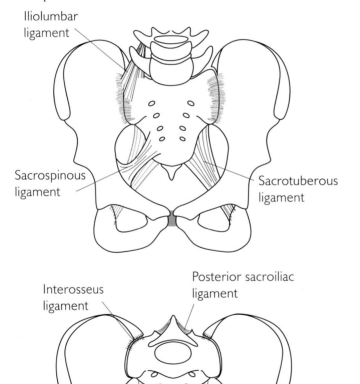

Figure 2.2

Ligaments of the pelvis

Perhaps at this stage it is useful to remind ourselves of the normal appearance and radiographic anatomy of the pelvis.

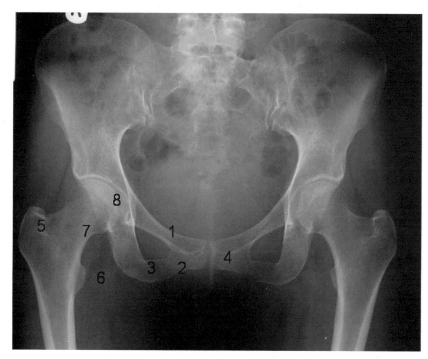

1. Superior pubic ramus
2. Inferior pubic ramus
3. Ischial tuberosity
4. Symphysis pubis
5. Greater trochanter
6. Lesser trochanter
7. Femoral neck
8. Femoral head

Figure 2.3 **Normal appearance of the pelvis**

What to look for on an anterior posterior radiograph of a trauma pelvis

As with any radiograph you should trace round all the cortices, looking for breaks or steps in the cortex associated with a lucent or sclerotic line.

Certain other areas of the pelvis radiograph require careful attention:

- Note the width and symmetry of the sacroiliac joints – there may be an occult fracture.
- Check the relative height of the iliac wings – one higher than the other may be a sign of vertical shear injury.
- Look for a fracture of the transverse processes of lumbar vertebra 5, which may be associated with an underlying fracture around the sacroiliac joints (remember where the iliolumbar and lumbosacral ligaments are located).
- Check the status of the foraminal lines within the sacrum, which serve as a clue to the presence of fracture of the sacral ala (compare one side to the other).

- Check the iliopubic and ilioischial lines for any steps/irregularities which may be indicative of a subtle acetabulum fracture.
- Beware of normal accessory ossicles, such as the Os acetabuli, not to be confused with an avulsion. Remember ossicles are normally well corticated and you cannot see a donor site for them.
- The vascular Y groove of the ilium should not be confused with a fracture; it has a fine margin of bony sclerosis.
- In children, remember the Y-shaped tri-radiate cartilage of the acetabulum.
- Check that the superior aspects of the symphysis pubis align, and that the joint is no more than 5mm wide.

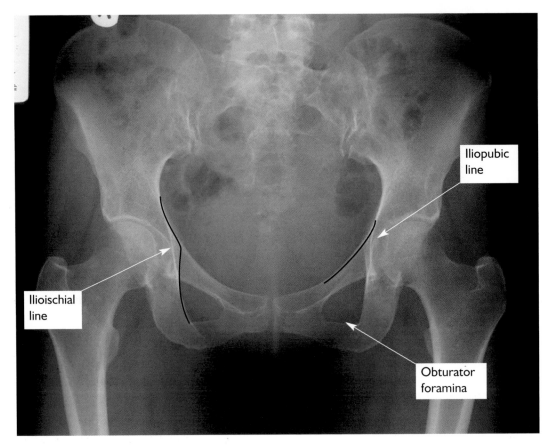

Figure 2.4 **Iliopubic and ilioischial lines**

Remember: if you see a fracture anteriorly, look extra carefully posteriorly.

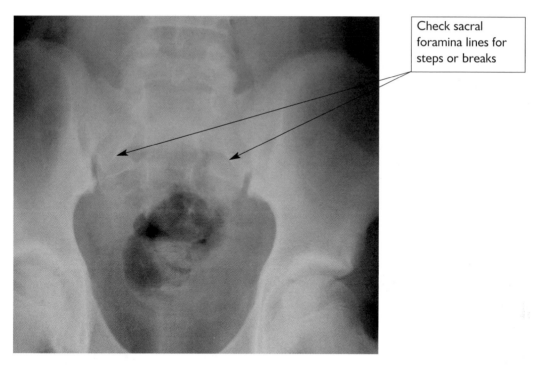

Check sacral foramina lines for steps or breaks

Figure 2.5 **Sacral foramina lines**

Types of pelvic fracture

Until recently it was thought that low impact forces could create fractures of the pelvis limited to the anterior arch (which is the weakest of the two main arches). Growing clinical evidence shows that this is not the case; fractures of the pubic rami are associated with fractures or ligamentous injuries in or about the acetabulum or sacroiliac joints, as confirmed by computerised axial tomography (CT).

Stability of the pelvis is dependent upon the integrity of the anterior and posterior arch. Disruption through joints, ligaments or bone in both the anterior and posterior arches of the pelvis results in instability. The greater the disruption, the greater the instability. But the ligaments holding the pelvis together allow some flexibility in the pelvis; so there may be a fracture anteriorly affecting the pelvic ring, whereas the posterior injury may be a ligamentous injury; as in the case of osteoporotic/elderly ladies who have solitary pubic or ischial rami fractures. Consequently pelvic fracture can be divided into two sorts: those that affect the pelvic ring and those that do not. First we will briefly comment on stable pelvic fractures.

Stable fractures that do not affect the pelvic ring

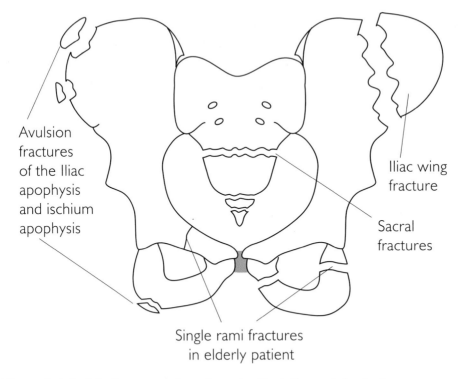

Avulsion fractures of the Iliac apophysis and ischium apophysis

Iliac wing fracture

Sacral fractures

Single rami fractures in elderly patient

Figure 2.6 **Stable fractures that do not affect the pelvic ring**

- Single ramus fractures – solitary pubic or ischial rami fractures. Commonly seen in older patients secondary to minor falls, half of pubic rami fractures are located near the medial margin of the obturator foramen.
- Ischial body fractures – direct blow to the ischium, such as a fall in a sitting position, a rare pelvic fracture.
- Iliac wing fractures (Duverney) – normally caused by a direct blow, it is important to distinguish between these and acetabulum fractures involving the iliac wing. The second type of fracture would involve the pelvic ring, while the first would not and hence they require different management.
- Sacral fractures – normally caused by a direct blow, often radiographically occult, especially in osteoporotic patients. Complications include tearing of exiting nerve roots, perineal parathesia, incontinence, cerebrospinal fluid leak, rectal laceration.

Fractures that do involve the pelvic ring

Tile and Pennel divided fractures of the pelvis involving the pelvic ring into three categories based on the mechanism of injury: lateral compression (the most common mechanism of injury), anterior compression and vertical shear. If the mechanism of injury is shown, it can be inferred which ligaments are placed under tension and potentially torn.

Lateral compression

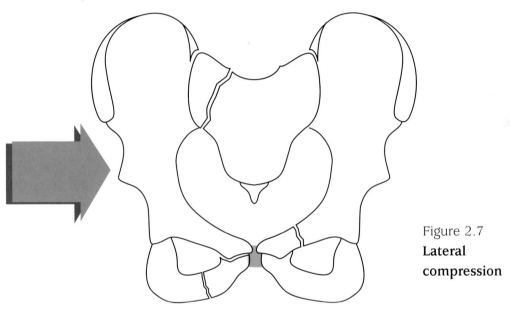

Figure 2.7
Lateral compression

A direct lateral blow to the iliac crest creates a force parallel to the ipsilateral rami, which compresses and fractures them (often involving superior and inferior pubic rami). Frequently the pubic fractures run in the horizontal or coronal plane. Although the anterior articular surfaces of the sacrum and ilium are compressed together and may fracture, the anterior and posterior sacroiliac ligaments remain intact, so posterior stability is retained. Often the impacted fractures around the sacroiliac joints are occult (look carefully at the foraminal lines within the sacrum, comparing one side with the other), but are demonstrated on CT. More severe lateral compression may result in disruption of the posterior ligament complex, resulting in instability and vascular damage. On occasions lateral compression injury may result in disruption of the ligamentous complex and widening of the sacroiliac joint posteriorly without an associated fracture of the sacrum.

15

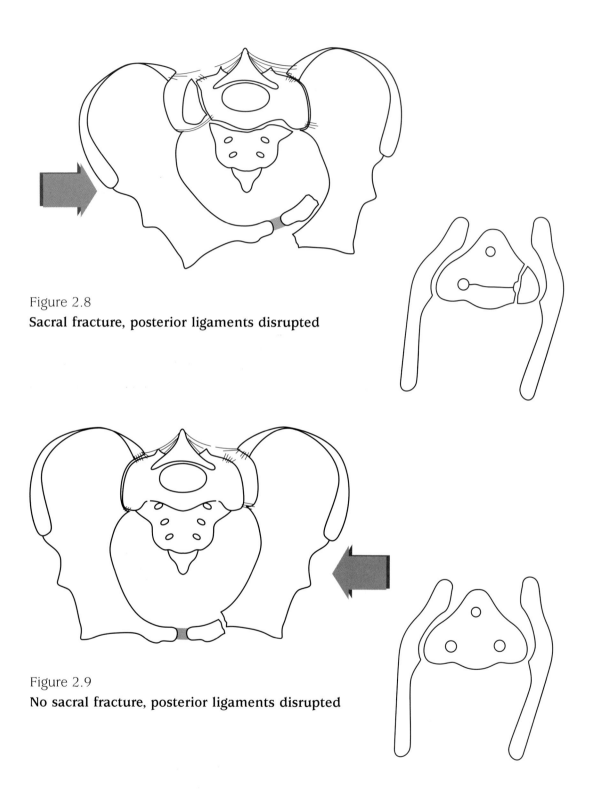

Figure 2.8
Sacral fracture, posterior ligaments disrupted

Figure 2.9
No sacral fracture, posterior ligaments disrupted

Anterior compression

Anterior compression of both of the anterior superior iliac spines causes diastasis of the symphysis pubis (some may refer to this as open book or sprung pelvis). The mildest injury separates the symphysis pubis or fractures the rami on one side only. Further opening of the symphysis pubis of more than 2.5 cm results in significant disruption of the anterior sacroiliac ligaments, but leaves the posterior sacroiliac ligaments intact. Greater anterior compression may disrupt the posterior ligaments as well.

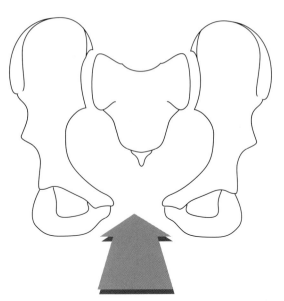

Figure 2.10 **Anterior compression**

This may be demonstrated on the pelvis radiograph by widening of the sacroiliac joints unilaterally or bilaterally. When these ligaments are disrupted it can on occasion result in lateral rotation of one of the innominate bones, demonstrated on the pelvic radiograph by one innominate bone appearing wider than the other. This demonstrates the importance (although this may be difficult) of obtaining a straight trauma pelvis, to allow comparison of one side of the pelvis to the other.

Occasionally the posterior aspect of this injury may be a fracture through the anterior margin of the ilium due to avulsion by the anterior sacro ligaments.

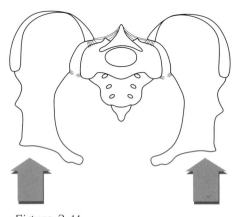

Figure 2.11
Anterior ligaments disrupted, posterior ligaments intact

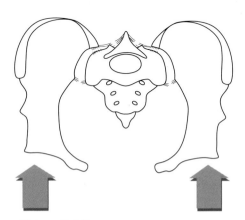

Figure 2.12
Anterior ligaments and posterior ligaments disrupted

17

Vertical shear

This type of fracture was classically described by Malgaigne in 1855 following being run over by a horse and cart (40 years before x-rays). Today it typically occurs following road traffic accidents, falls from a height, or industrial injuries. Forces are transmitted by the femur to the acetabulum, resulting in vertical displacement of the ipsilateral hemipelvis. Vertical displacement results in fracture of the ipsilateral sacral ala and pubic rami.

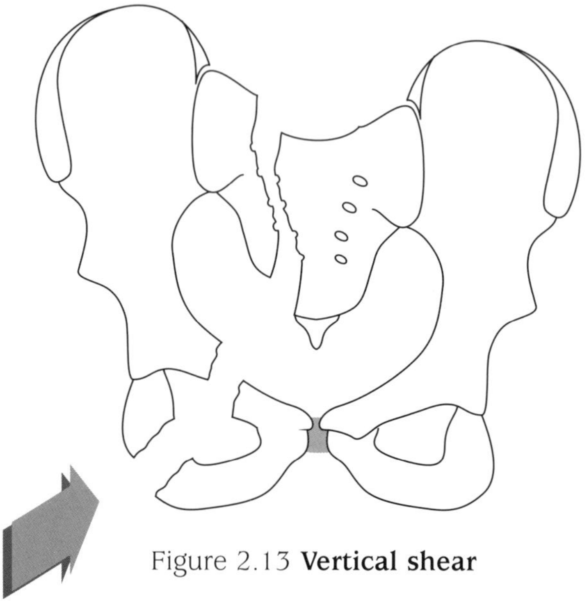

Figure 2.13 **Vertical shear**

Characterised anteriorly by bilateral pubic rami fractures or symphysis diastasis (widening), with dramatic posterior disruption either through the sacroiliac joint or through the ilium or sacrum, the injury pushes the hemipelvis medially and superiorly. With the anterior tilt of the pelvis, any force pushing the hemipelvis superiorly will also push it posteriorly in relation to the sacrum. Inlet and outlet views are frequently used in initial evaluation of this injury. The inlet view will demonstrate the posterior displacement of the hemipelvis, whereas the outlet view shows its superior displacement. Medial displacement is demonstrated on any of the views. In our trust, inlet and outlet views are used in initial evaluation of lateral and anterior compression injuries (as well) and in follow up of these injuries post surgery. As well as demonstrating displacement, the outlet view can be useful in assessing rami fracture (as shown below), as the cephalad angulation opens up the rami, allowing clear radiographic visualisation. Both inlet and outlet views can help identify occult sacral fractures. Following initial radiographs these injuries normally have CT to demonstrate the extent of injuries and help in planning surgery.

Frequently in vertical shear the iliolumbar ligament avulses the ipsilateral transverse process of lumbar vertebra 5, as the iliac bone travels cephalad. These are very unstable injuries and have a high rate of vascular damage.

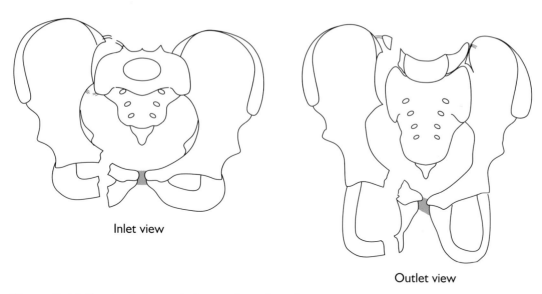

Inlet view

Outlet view

Figure 2.14 **Vertical shear, inlet and outlet views**

Vertical shear can appear similar radiographically and clinically to severe lateral compression injuries, in which the hemipelvis may be displaced slightly cephalad and rotated medially; both present with a foreshortened internally rotated ipsilateral lower extremity. However, in the vertical shear the vertically directed force dominates. The posterior displacement of the injured hemipelvis in vertical shear results in torn anterior and posterior sacroiliac ligaments, whereas lateral compression injury normally spares the anterior sacroiliac ligaments.

Conclusion

The pelvis is a ring-ike structure; if a fracture disrupts the ring, then look for another injury – it may be ligamentous. Some injuries to the pelvis may be difficult to see radiographically, requiring additional projections. Understanding the mechanisms of injury may assist in the search for occult pelvic injuries.

3.

Reviewing cervical spine radiographs

Karen Sakthivel-Wainford

Anatomy

The cervical spine is made up of seven vertebrae, held together by a series of ligaments and paravertebral muscles, which influence the stability of the spine.

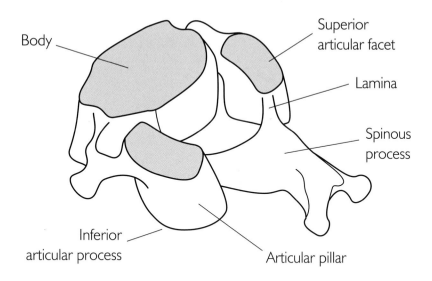

Figure 3.1
The cervical vertebra

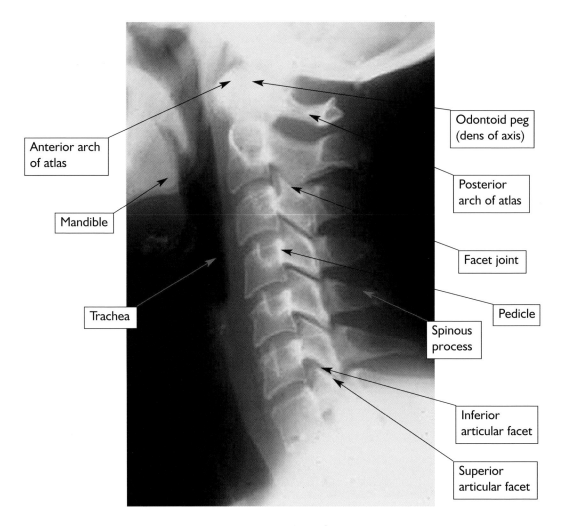

Figure 3.2 **Cervical vertebrae, lateral view**

Ligaments

The anterior longitudinal ligament runs from the anterior arch of the atlas to the sacrum; the posterior longitudinal ligament connects the posterior aspect of the vertebral bodies. These two ligaments assist in maintaining vertebral alignment. The posterior ligamentous complex consists of the ligamentum flavum, the interspinous and supraspinous ligaments. The intertransverse ligaments connect the transverse processes and form the lateral column.

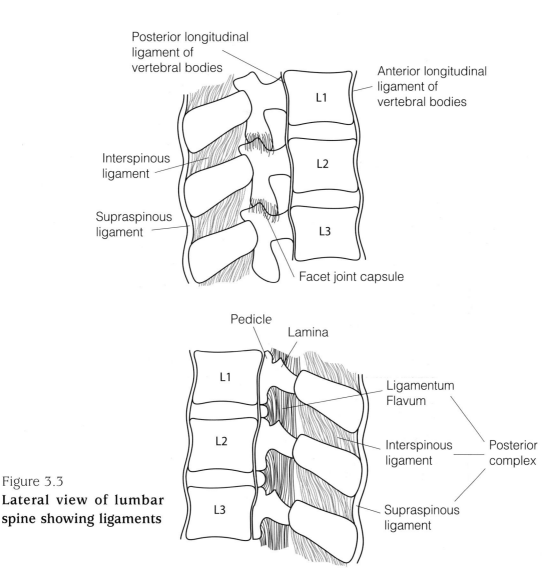

Figure 3.3
Lateral view of lumbar spine showing ligaments

The lateral radiograph

Assessing alignment on the lateral radiograph

This is normally the first radiograph to be taken, frequently taken in the resuscitation room with a hard collar in situ. It is the most important view for assessing vertebral alignment, with the use of several separate anteriorly convex arcs in the cervical spine (texts vary about the number of lines used from three to five – for completeness all five will be mentioned).

23

- Anterior spinal line – formed by joining the anterior margins of the vertebral bodies
- Posterior spinal line – formed by joining the posterior margins of the vertebral bodies
- Spinolaminar line – formed by joining the anterior margin of the junction of the laminae and spinous process
- Posterior pillar line – joins the posterior surface of the facet joints
- Spinous line – an additional line connecting the spinous process. Some authors comment that this line is not very useful, but it does help to focus attention on this area.

The lateral radiograph should include from the cranio-cervical junction to the upper border of thoracic vertebra 1. If the lower aspects of the cervical spine are not clearly demonstrated then alternative projections should be carried out (this is frequently a swimmer's view), but in some departments trauma obliques are an alternative.

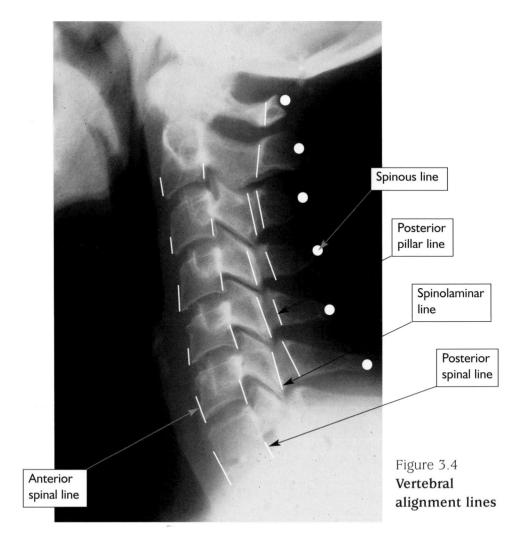

Spinous line

Posterior pillar line

Spinolaminar line

Posterior spinal line

Anterior spinal line

Figure 3.4
Vertebral alignment lines

Also check the distance between adjacent vertebral bodies; they should be parallel with no widening. The anterior arch of cervical vertebra 1 should be no more than 2.5mm away from the dens, except in children where the distance will be 5mm. The facet joints should be aligned (like tiles on a roof).

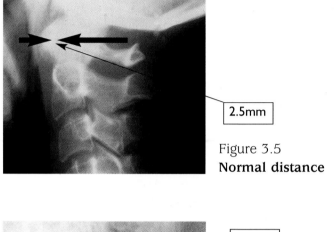

2.5mm

Figure 3.5
Normal distance

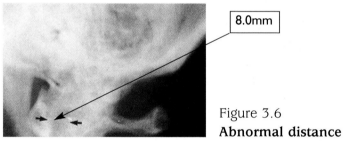

8.0mm

Figure 3.6
Abnormal distance

Soft tissues on lateral radiograph

The prevertebral soft tissue in adults is not more than 5mm at C3 and C4, and less than 22mm at C6. It is not always easy to measure these distances, particularly if you do not know whether the image you are viewing is life size. Alternatively prevertebral distance at C1–4 is equal to the intervertebral distance, and equal to a vertebral body width below C5.

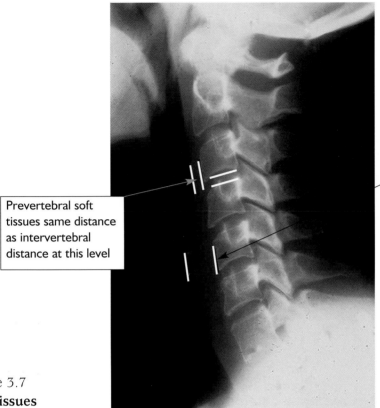

Prevertebral soft tissue same distance at this level as vertebra

Prevertebral soft tissues same distance as intervertebral distance at this level

Figure 3.7
Soft tissues

The antero-posterior radiograph

Antero-posterior and the open mouth view are required to clear the cervical spine of trauma. They are often taken later than the lateral radiograph, when the patient has been stabilised. Antero-posterior radiographs should include from cervical vertebra 2/3 to cervical vertebra 7. The spinous processes should be in a straight line, with the distance between each spinous process roughly equal. If the spinous process line deviates from its normal straight line this is indicative of unilateral facet dislocation. Widening of the interspinous distance occurs in an anterior cervical dislocation or posterior ligament rupture.

A bifid spinous process may be demonstrated on the antero-posterior radiograph. In Clay shoveller's fracture (fracture of spinous process, normally C7) a 'double' spinous process is seen.

The lateral aspects of the cervical vertebra should also be carefully checked for fracture.

26

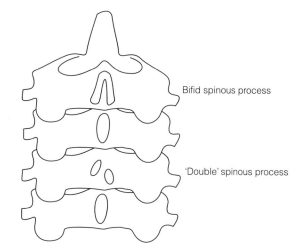

Figure 3.8

Diagrammatic representation of bifid spinous process and Clay shoveller's fracture (double spinous process) as demonstrated on the antero-posterior radiograph

The open mouth view

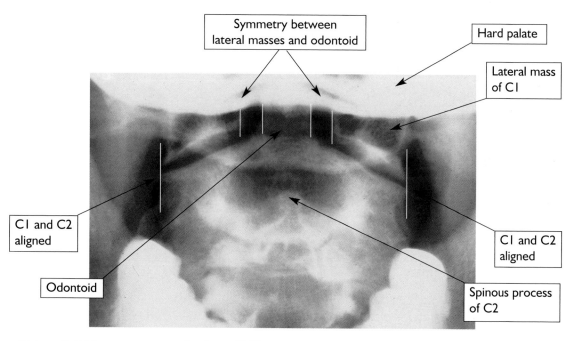

Figure 3.9 **The open mouth view (OM)**

The open mouth view is difficult to obtain with hard collar in situ and oxygen mask (the latter may sometimes be removed for the second the x-ray is taken, following discussion with the doctor). The radiograph should show the C1/C2 articulation and odontoid peg clearly. The lateral masses of C1 should align with the lateral margins of C2. Check also for symmetry between the odontoid peg and lateral masses of C2. This requires a non-rotated radiograph, which may require the assistance of the clinician if the patient's neck has been placed obliquely in the hard collar.

Beware of the 'mach effect': the occiput may overshadow the odontoid process, simulating a fracture. Teeth may also overlie the occiput, causing confusing shadows.

Main mechanisms of injury

These include hyperflexion, hyperflexion and rotation, hyperextension, hyperextension and rotation and compression injuries. Generally each mechanism of injury gives characteristic types of fracture (some of which will be demonstrated in the cases). The cervical spine is injured when subjected to a series of forces acting separately or in combination. A common area of injury is C1/2 following impaction with the skull base. C5–7 is also a common area of injury. Remember: it is common to have multiple fractures of the cervical spine, so if you see one fracture always look for another (one injury may be upper cervical spine while the other is lower cervical spine).

Hyperflexion injuries
- Hyperflexion sprain
- Clay shoveller's fracture
- Anterior wedge fracture
- Bilateral facet dislocation
- Unilateral facet dislocation (hyperflexion with rotation)
- Teardrop burst fracture.

Hyperextension injuries
- Hangman's fracture
- Hyperextension sprain
- Extension teardrop fracture
- Hyperextension fracture dislocation (hyperextension rotation, with some compression).

Axial compression
- Jefferson's fracture
- Burst fracture.

Indeterminate mechanism
- Odontoid process fractures.

The ABCS in cervical trauma

Many texts talk about ABCS when reviewing trauma; this method can also assist in reviewing cervical radiographs. As a reminder:

A = Alignment

B = Bone integrity

C = Cartilage

S = Soft tissues

Alignment

- Disrupted cervical arcs
- Focal kyphosis/scoliosis
- Spinous process rotation
- Widening of interpedicular distance
- Loss of cervical lordosis
- Vertebral listhesis.

Bone integrity

- Fracture
- Cortical buckling
- Wedged vertebra
- Disrupted CV2.

Cartilage (joint) space

- Facet joint widening
- Interspinous widening ('fanning')
- Widened predental space
- Widened intervertebral disc space.

Soft tissues

- Widened prevertebral space

The advantage of this systematic approach to reviewing the radiographs is that it provides a list of clues to injury, which is particularly helpful to the inexperienced reporter.

Radiographic signs of cervical instability

- Widening of intervertebral disc space
- Spinous process fanning
- Angulation greater than 11 degrees
- Horizontal displacement of one vertebral body on another by more than 3.5mm
- Facet joint widening, facet joint overriding
- Multiple fractures – remember if you see one fracture of the cervical spine, look for another.

When reviewing cervical spine radiographs it is useful to have a set method of reviewing, as suggested above. For example, first check alignment, bony integrity, joint spaces, normal distances between bony anatomy, then soft tissues. Also try to familiarise yourself with all the above injuries.

4.

Pelvic trauma

Case 1

Elderly patient fell from step while washing windows.

Now pain in right hip area.

Is there a fracture?

If so how common is this injury?

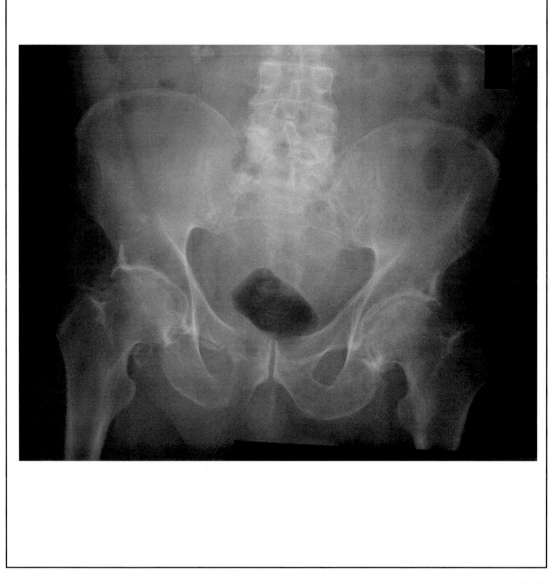

Answer to Case 1

There are fractures of the right superior and inferior pubic rami, close to the medial aspect of the obturator foramen. As mentioned in Chapter 2, over half of the fractures of the pubic rami are located close to the medial aspect of the obturator foramen. Pubic rami fractures commonly occur in the elderly following minor falls, and form about 22 % of pelvic fractures.

Case 2

Young cyclist involved in a road traffic accident.

Describe the radiograph.

Would any further radiographic views be helpful?

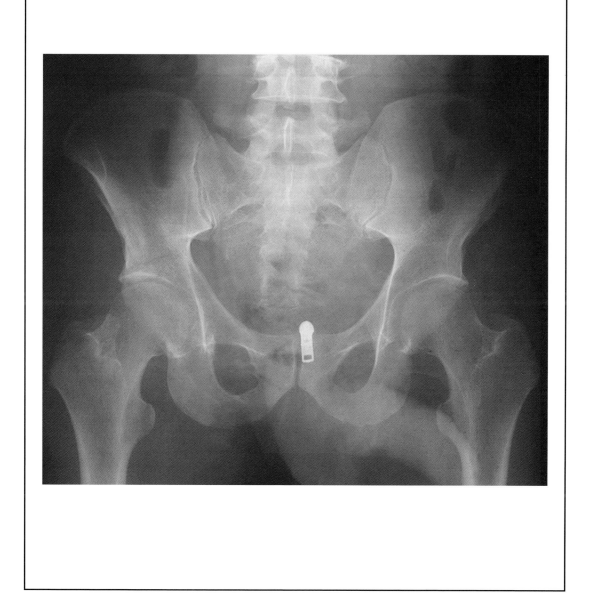

Answer to Case 2

The pelvis radiograph demonstrates a fracture of the right inferior pubic rami, just lateral to the symphysis pubis, again near the medial aspect of the obturator foramen.

This is not an elderly patient, or a minor trauma, and as the pelvis acts as a bony ring, the rest of the pelvis needs to be reviewed for further fracture. Superior to the right acetabulum is a transverse lucent line, which is probably a fracture. There is a slight bulge at the right iliopubic line, which can be indicative of a fracture of the acetabulum. Following review of the radiograph, Judet's views were performed, to confirm/rule out fracture of acetabulum, and demonstrate the lucent line superior to acetabulum.

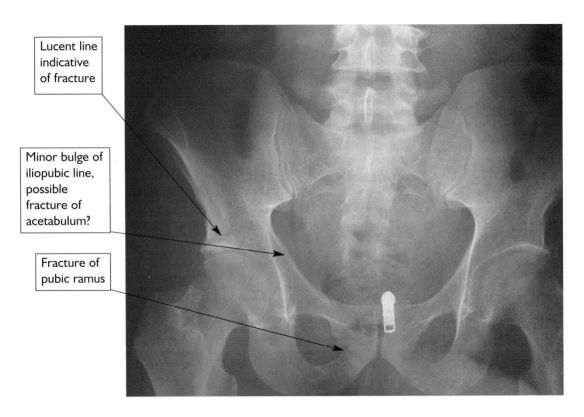

Lucent line indicative of fracture

Minor bulge of iliopubic line, possible fracture of acetabulum?

Fracture of pubic ramus

Judet's views are radiographs taken to assess acetabular fracture, the patient being rotated 45 degrees one way then the other. These views are taken following guidance from the clinician, the patient being log rolled into position by experienced staff to prevent any further injury. In our trust, initial Judet's views include the whole pelvis to visualise any other possible fractures; follow-up Judet's views are collimated to the affected side.

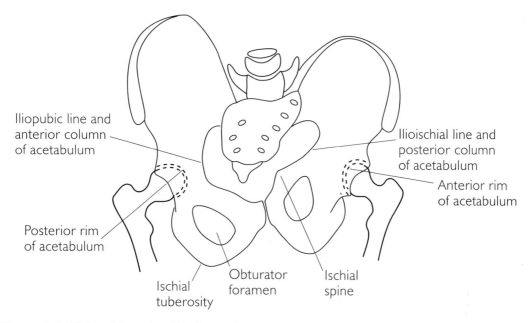

Iliopubic line and anterior column of acetabulum

Ilioischial line and posterior column of acetabulum

Anterior rim of acetabulum

Posterior rim of acetabulum

Ischial tuberosity

Obturator foramen

Ischial spine

Figure 4.1 **Right side raised Judet's view**

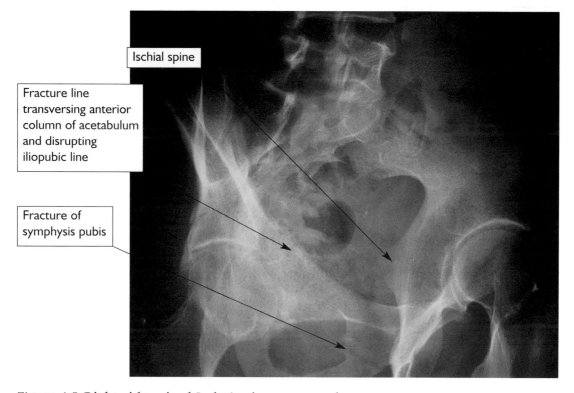

Ischial spine

Fracture line transversing anterior column of acetabulum and disrupting iliopubic line

Fracture of symphysis pubis

Figure 4.2 **Right side raised Judet's view – example**

37

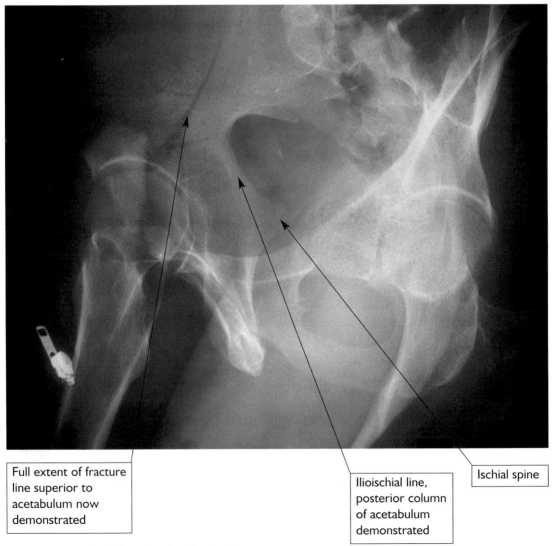

Full extent of fracture line superior to acetabulum now demonstrated

Ilioischial line, posterior column of acetabulum demonstrated

Ischial spine

Figure 4.3 **Left side raised Judet's view**

The Judet's views demonstrate the full extent of the fracture superior to the acetabulum, plus a fracture of the right acetabulum. Signs of pelvic fracture can often be subtle, requiring careful observation and a systematic approach to reviewing the radiograph (the list of points in Chapter 2 may be helpful). Additional projections may be useful in assessing these injuries.

Case 3

Patient fell on to right hip, now painful to walk.

Describe the radiograph.

Discuss the appearance of the pelvis.

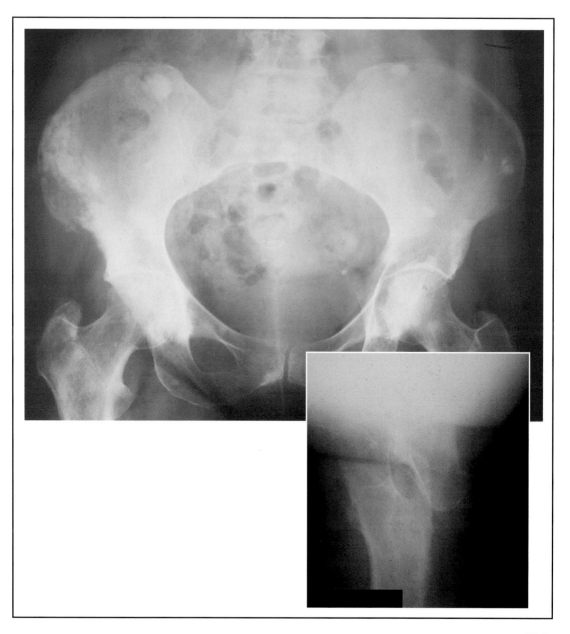

Answer to Case 3

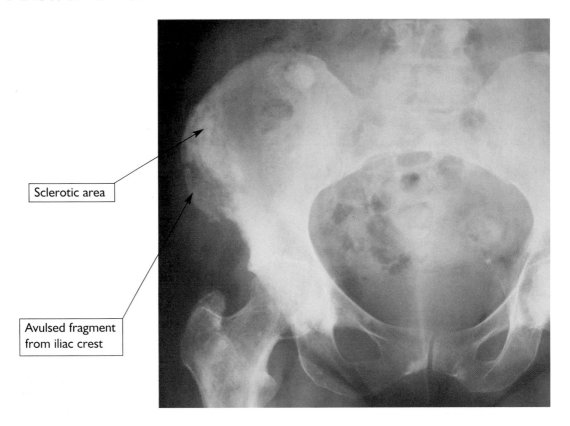

Sclerotic area

Avulsed fragment
from iliac crest

There is an avulsed fragment from the iliac crest. On review of the radiograph there are several sclerotic areas close to the avulsed fragment and around the acetabulum. The patient was undergoing cancer treatment. These sclerotic areas in the pelvis are secondary deposits; this is a pathological fracture.

Case 4

Patient was involved in a road traffic incident; pelvis was taken as part of a trauma series in the resuscitation room.

Describe the radiograph.

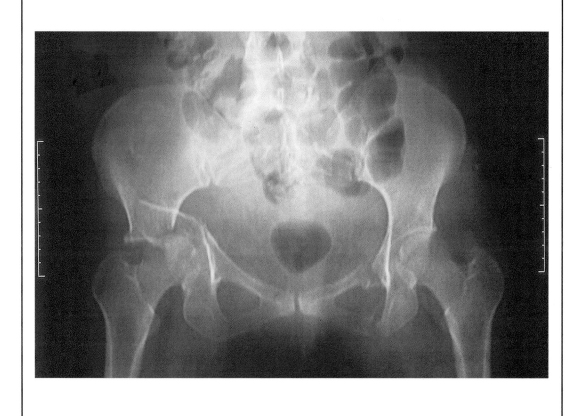

Answer to Case 4

There are readily demonstrated fractures of the left superior and inferior pubic rami, and comminuted fracture of the right acetabulum. The right sacroiliac joint is wider than the left, indicating injury to the sacroiliac ligaments. If you compare one ischium with the other, then the right ischium appears wider than the left. This is a good indication that the sacroiliac ligaments on the wider side have been damaged, hence allowing the ischium to rotate laterally, making it appear wider on the radiograph. It is always useful on a trauma pelvis radiograph to compare one ischium with the other. This of course requires a straight pelvis radiograph, which can be very challenging in the trauma setting.

Case 5

Patient was a passenger in a car that was involved in a side impact by another car.

Describe the radiograph.

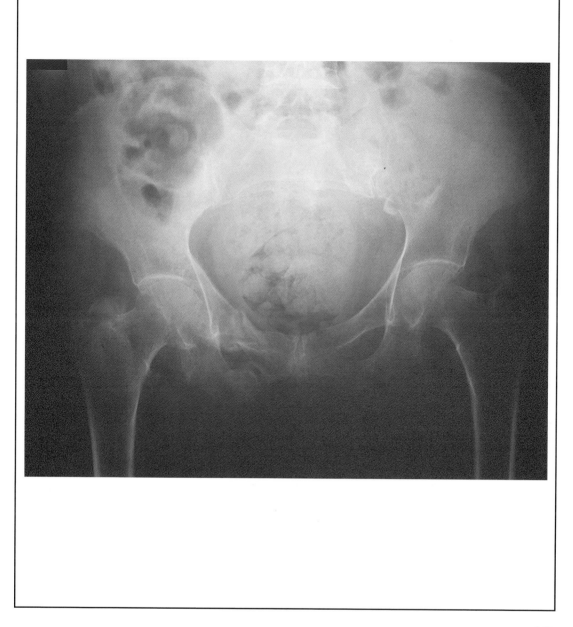

Answer to Case 5

There are several fractures: comminuted, impacted fractures of the right superior and inferior pubic rami. Remember, if you fracture the anterior pelvis to review the posterior structure. In this case the sacrum is covered with bowel gas and difficult to assess. There is a posterior fracture of the left ischium close to the sacroiliac joint. Also a fracture of the greater trochanter of the right hip is demonstrated. This was probably a lateral compression injury (see pages 15–16). The patient went for CT to further assess their injuries.

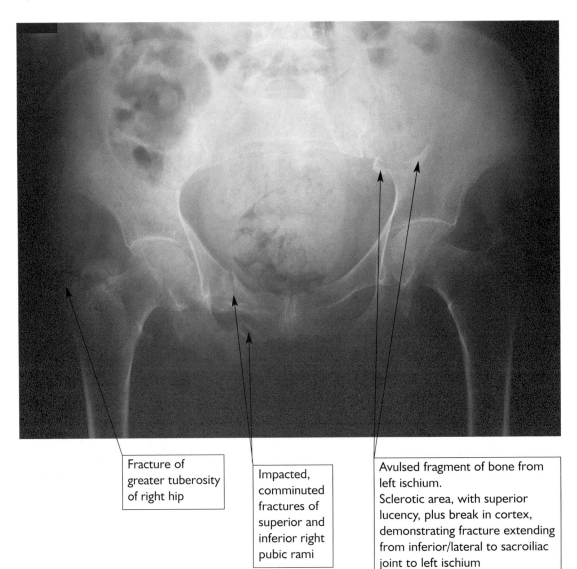

Fracture of greater tuberosity of right hip

Impacted, comminuted fractures of superior and inferior right pubic rami

Avulsed fragment of bone from left ischium.
Sclerotic area, with superior lucency, plus break in cortex, demonstrating fracture extending from inferior/lateral to sacroiliac joint to left ischium

Case 6

Patient was pedestrian hit by a car.

Describe the injuries.

What is the most likely mechanism of injury?

Which ligaments are most likely to be affected in this mechanism of injury?

Name the three main mechanisms of injury of the pelvis, as described by Tile and Pennel (1980).

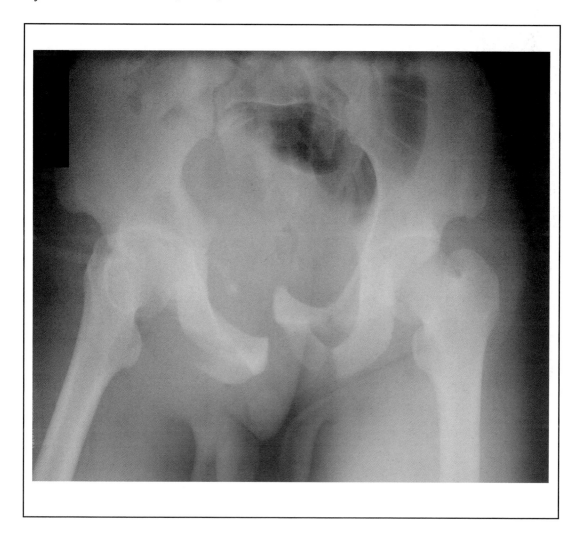

Answer to Case 6

There are fractures of the left superior and inferior pubic rami, and the right inferior pubic ramus (the right superior pubic ramus is not readily demonstrated). There is widening and malalignment of the symphysis pubis. In adults, if the symphysis pubis is widened by more than 2.5 cm then the anterior sacroiliac ligaments will be disrupted. On reviewing the radiograph there is widening of the right sacroiliac joint.

Also notice the right ischium is wider than the left. As the anterior sacroiliac ligaments are disrupted, the affected ischium can rotate laterally (in effect opening up the ischium on the affected side). This gives the appearance on the radiograph of one ischium being wider than the other. This highlights the necessity of producing as straight a trauma pelvic radiograph as possible.

This is an anterior compression injury. Tile and Pennel described: lateral compression injuries, anterior compression and vertical shear (see pages 15–19).

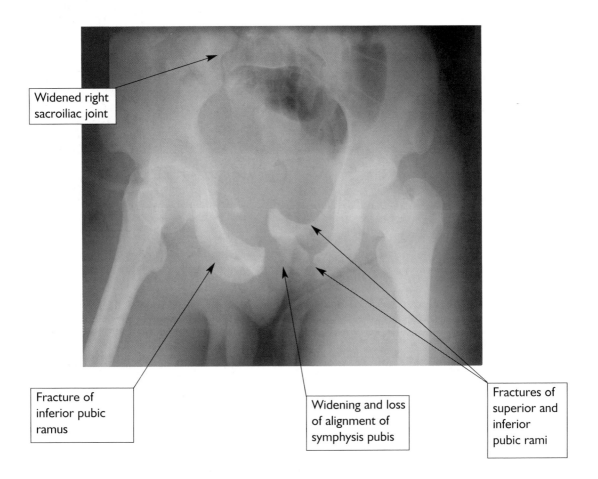

Widened right sacroiliac joint

Fracture of inferior pubic ramus

Widening and loss of alignment of symphysis pubis

Fractures of superior and inferior pubic rami

Case 7

Patient fell from a great height.

Describe the injuries.

What is the mechanism of injury?

Which ligaments around the sacroiliac joints are likely to be affected?

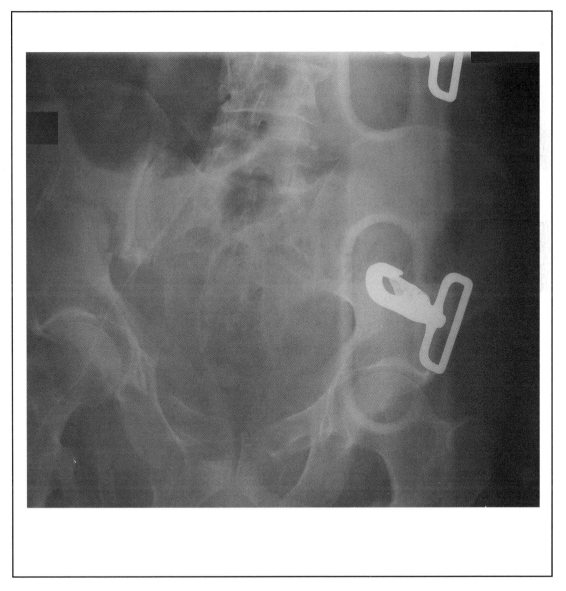

Answer to Case 7

There are fractures of the right superior and inferior pubic rami; there is an oblique fracture of the right ischium just lateral to the sacroiliac joint. The whole right hemipelvis appears to have moved vertically. This is a vertical shear type injury, which results in disruption of the anterior and posterior sacroiliac ligaments. The metal clips on the radiograph are from the spinal board that the patient is still on. Ideally the patient should be removed from the spinal board prior to x-ray.

Case 8

Patient fell in bathroom two weeks ago.

Pain in right hip increasing; now walking with great difficulty.

Describe the radiograph.

Would any further imaging be helpful?

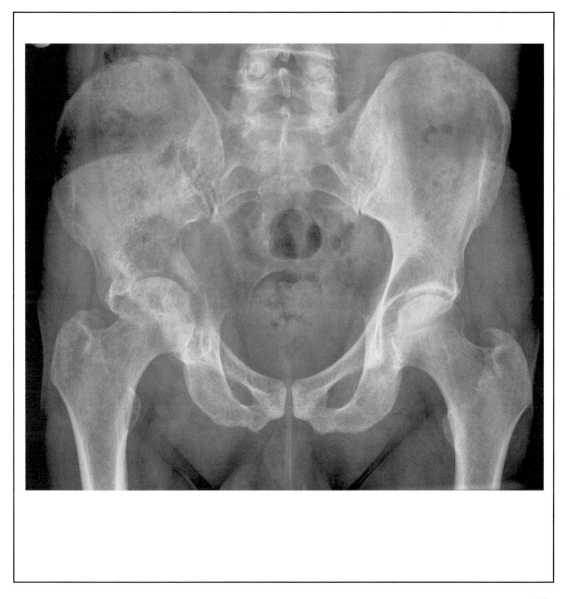

Answer to Case 8

There is a central comminuted fracture of the right acetabulum. The bone texture surrounding the acetabulum appears abnormally lytic – this is a pathological fracture.

Judet's views were taken, as shown.

Judet's views demonstrate there is loss of bone (lytic bone destruction) at the anterior and posterior columns of the acetabulum, which has resulted in a pathological fracture. CT was performed, which demonstrated further lytic deposits in the left

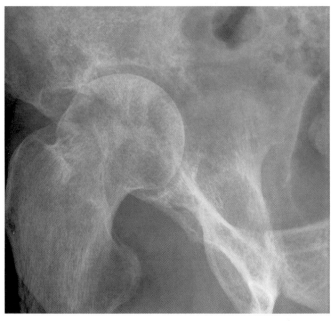

sacrum, right and left femoral heads and left acetabulum (which if it progresses may lead to another pathological fracture). It is important that pathological fractures are recognised and followed up with appropriate imaging – normally CT. If the pathology involves bone, CT is usually carried out to see the extent of the pathology in that locality

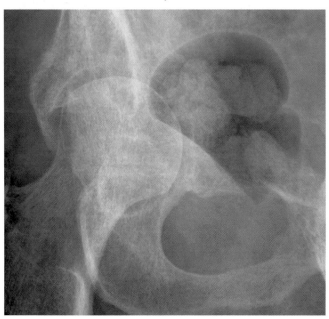

(in this case the pelvis), and also whether other areas are prone to pathological fracture, as sometimes, if recognised early, preventive orthopaedic fixation may take place. Often a bone scan is taken to assess the spread of the tumour/pathology and sometimes to locate the primary tumour. Where the pathology involves soft tissues, an MRI scan may be performed to assess the extent of the pathology.

Case 9

Patient fell down stone steps on to pelvis.

Describe the injuries.

Would any other radiographs be helpful?

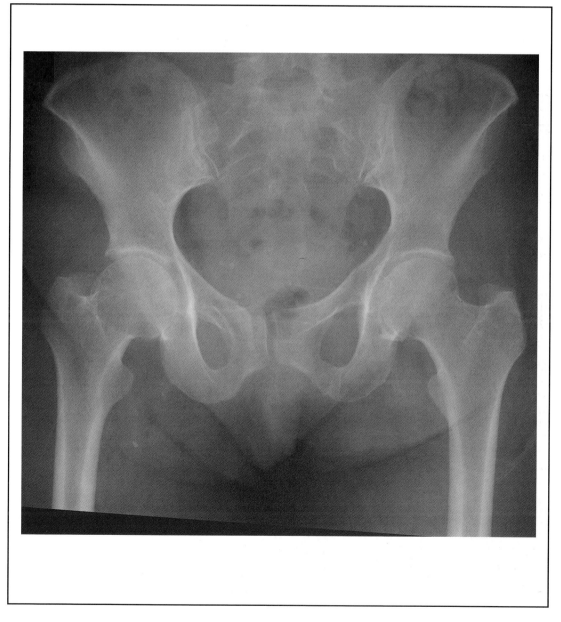

Answer to Case 9

There are fractures of the inferior and superior pubic rami bilaterally; there is a bulge in the left iliopubic line, which may be indicative of an acetabulum fracture. The pelvis is a bony ring; if you see fractures involving the anterior pelvis look posteriorly, especially at the sacral area (also review the acetabular area). This radiograph demonstrates disruption of the left sacral alar. Judet's views would be useful to further assess the left acetabulum; ideally in trauma both Judet's views should be taken to assess acetabulum columns and rim (see Chapter 2). In this case there is only one Judet's view available.

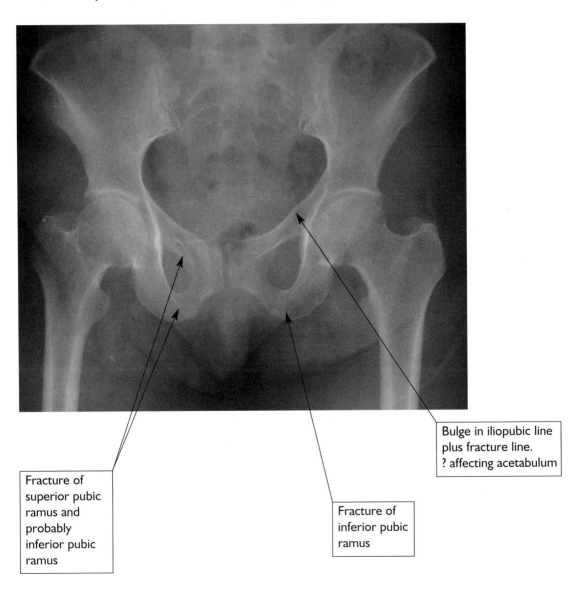

Bulge in iliopubic line plus fracture line. ? affecting acetabulum

Fracture of superior pubic ramus and probably inferior pubic ramus

Fracture of inferior pubic ramus

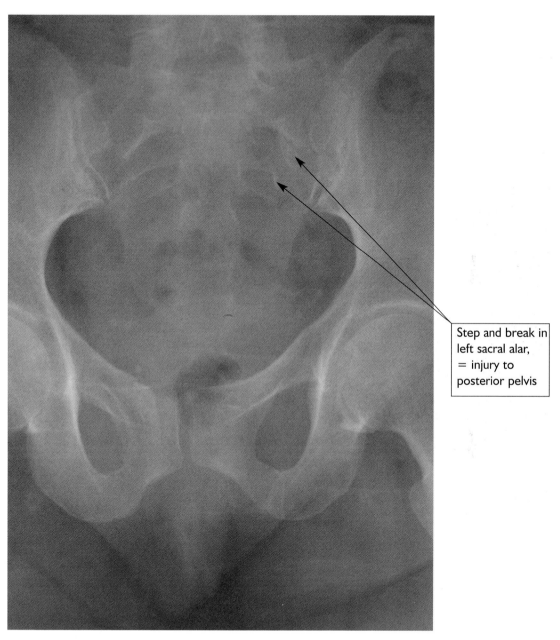

Step and break in left sacral alar, = injury to posterior pelvis

Magnified sacrum from pelvic radiograph

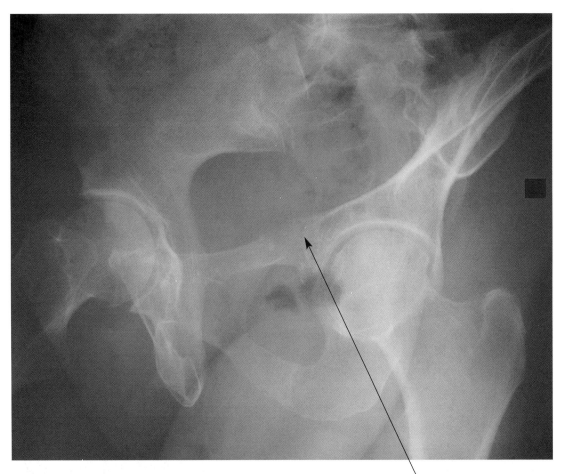

Judet's view left side raised

Fracture line involving iliopubic line and anterior column of acetabulum

Case 10

Patient involved in a road traffic accident.

Describe the radiograph.

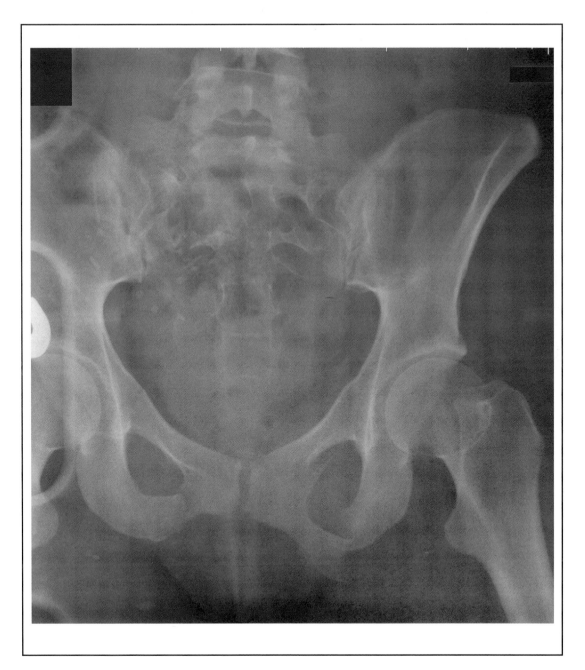

Answer to Case 10

There are bilateral fractures of the inferior and superior pubic rami; these are displaced on the left. The fracture of the left superior pubic ramus appears horizontal in orientation, which is classic in a lateral compression type of injury. The fracture of the right superior pubic ramus, appears to be leading to a bulging of the iliopubic line which may be indicative of an acetabular fracture. As previously mentioned, if fractures are demonstrated in the anterior pelvis, review the posterior pelvis. This radiograph demonstrates fractures of the right sacral alar. The spinal board is also seen on the radiograph. Not all the pelvis is demonstrated on this radiograph, but the patient was taken to theatre, prior to any repeats.

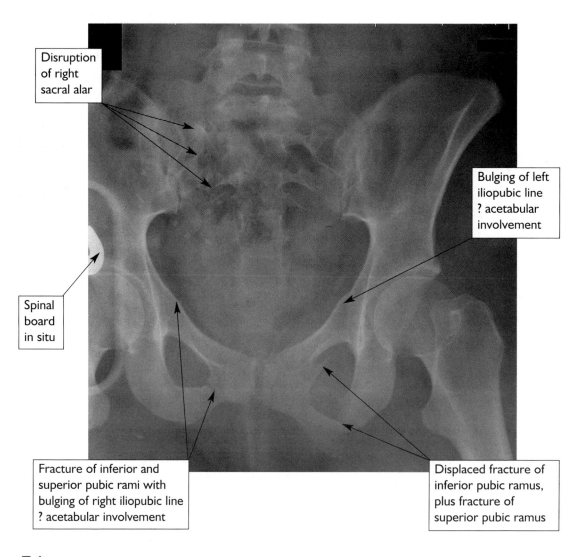

Disruption of right sacral alar

Bulging of left iliopubic line ? acetabular involvement

Spinal board in situ

Fracture of inferior and superior pubic rami with bulging of right iliopubic line ? acetabular involvement

Displaced fracture of inferior pubic ramus, plus fracture of superior pubic ramus

Case 11

Patient fell off bicycle.

Describe the radiograph.

Is there a fracture or an accessory ossicle present?

What clues can help in distinguishing one from the other?

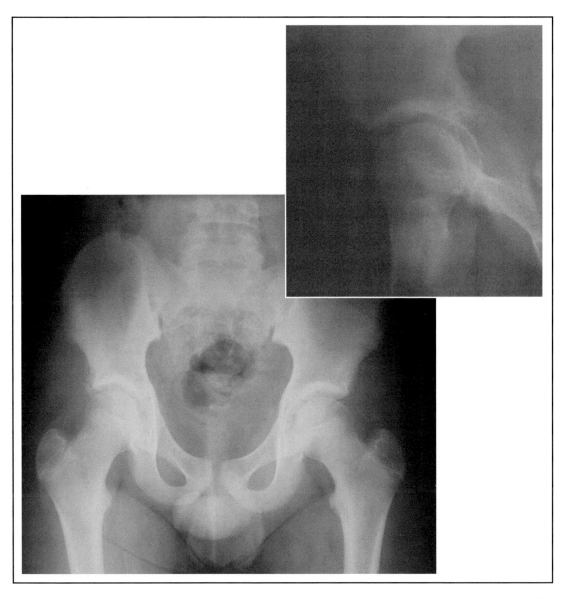

Answer to Case 11

There is an avulsion from the anterior iliac spine. By comparing both hips it is demonstrated that there is no such area on the left hip. However, there is a normal accessory ossicle sometimes found in this area called the os acetabulum. Accessory ossicles are normally well corticated and rounded (difficult to assess this on this pelvic radiograph). The lateral radiograph, however, demonstrates the bony fragment anterior to the acetabulum, confirming it is an avulsion not an accessory ossicle. Notice the normal tri-radiate cartilage of the acetabulum on these radiographs.

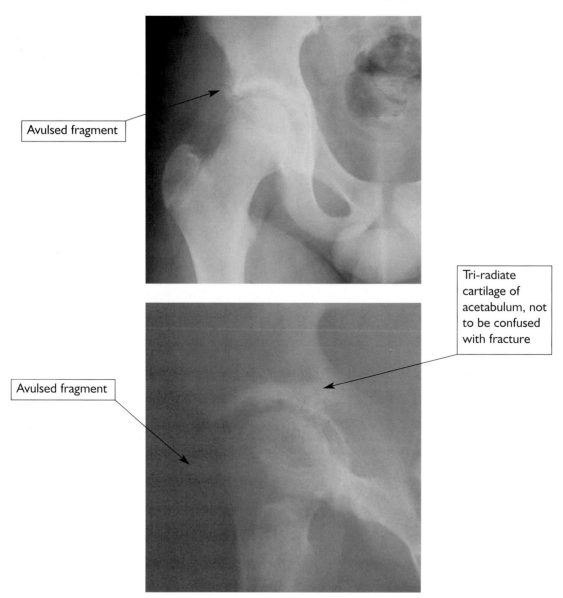

Avulsed fragment

Tri-radiate cartilage of acetabulum, not to be confused with fracture

Avulsed fragment

Case 12

Cheerleader fell awkwardly, now painful left hip.

Describe the radiographs. Is there an injury?

If so, what ligament is involved?

In what age group do these injuries of the pelvis commonly occur?

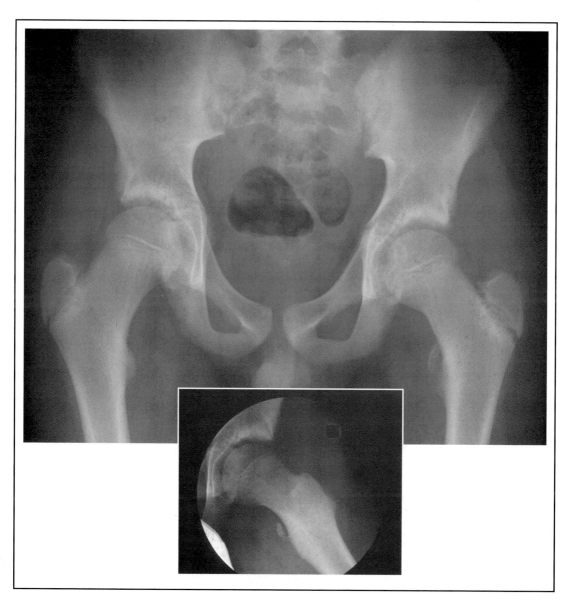

Answer to Case 12

There is an avulsion of the left lesser trochanter of the left hip (compare one side to the other). Avulsions of the apophyses of the pelvis are common between twelve and sixteen years of age. They commonly occur in long-jumpers, sprinters, gymnasts and cheerleaders. The ligament involved in this case is the iliopsoas. The diagram below shows the avulsions of the apophyses that may occur in the pelvis and their attached ligaments. The apophyses are weaker than the ligaments, hence are avulsed during trauma; the same injury occurring in an adult would probably result in tearing of the ligament. Remember the apophyses of the pelvis are the last to fuse at twenty-five years of age, so avulsions may potentially occur until this age.

One of the most commonly avulsed apophyses is at the ischial tuberosity, where the hamstrings attach. When an avulsion occurs here it often lays down lots of bone, which if sufficient can trap the sciatic nerve in later life, causing problems sitting down. The gross amount of bone laid down may be mistaken for osteomyelitis or Ewing's sarcoma, so care is required – there may not be a history of trauma.

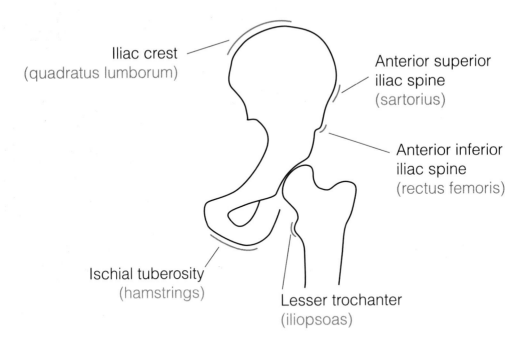

Figure 4.4 **Common sites of apophyseal avulsion and muscle attachment**

Case 13

Elderly patient fell from commode, now painful left hip.

Describe the radiograph.

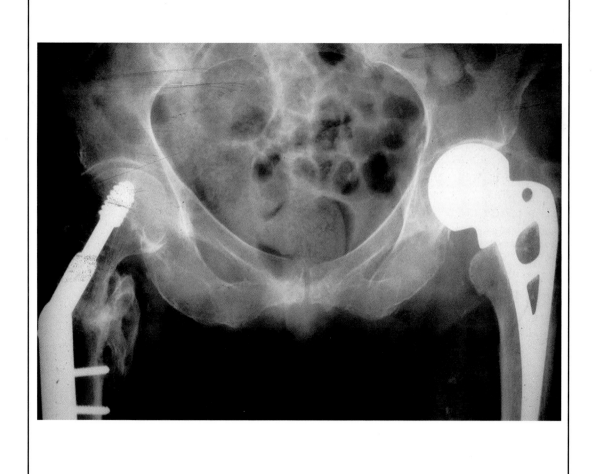

Answer to Case 13

There is a fracture of the left inferior pubic ramus, which as discussed in Chapter 2 is a common injury in the elderly, often following minor trauma.

The patient also has a right dynamic hip screw, following an intertrochanteric fracture (see page 82), and a left hemiarthroplasty following an intracapsular fracture of the femoral neck. The right lesser trochanter can be seen still detached from the femur. If metal work is in situ in the hip the radiograph needs to demonstrate the whole length of the metal work, as fractures often occur just distal to it.

Case 14

Patient fell down a flight of stairs.

Describe the injuries.

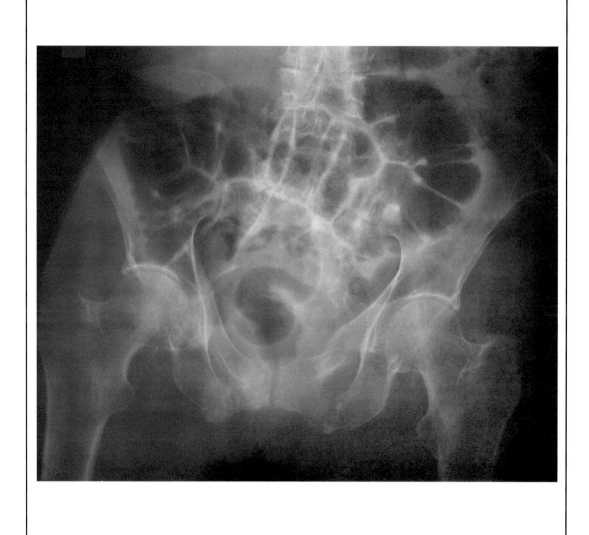

Answer to Case 14

There are comminuted fractures of the left superior and inferior pubic rami. The right inferior and superior pubic rami are also fractured, the superior fracture lying close to the midline. There is slight bulging of the right iliopubic line, which may be indicative of an acetabular fracture, requiring further investigation. This is an elderly patient, and the fracture of pubic rami are so severe that there are likely to be accompanying fractures of the acetabulum or posterior pelvis. There is a lot of bowel gas present, preventing clear visualisation of the posterior pelvis. CT was carried out to further assess the injuries.

Case 15

Patient fell on to hip, right leg now internally rotated and patient unable to weight bear.

Describe the radiograph.

Would another radiographic view be helpful?

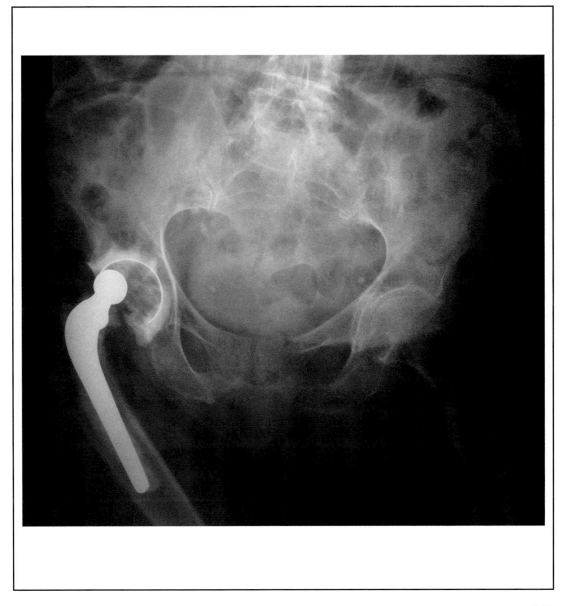

Answer to Case 15

The right hip has a total hip replacement in situ. There is loss of congruence of the acetabulum with the head of the replacement, indicative of dislocation. Hips normally dislocate posteriorly, resulting in an internally rotated leg (whereas a fractured neck of femur normally results in an externally rotated leg). Also note the shaft of the replacement no longer lies parallel to the bony shaft of the femur; more of the cement at the medial distal aspect of the replacement is visualised than normal. A lateral view confirms that the hip replacement has dislocated posteriorly.

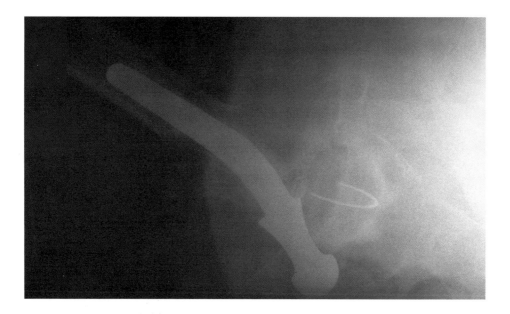

5.

Hip and femur trauma

7

Case 16

Patient fell down several steps, now unable to weight bear, painful left hip.

Describe the radiograph.

What radiographic line can be useful when looking for fractured neck of femur?

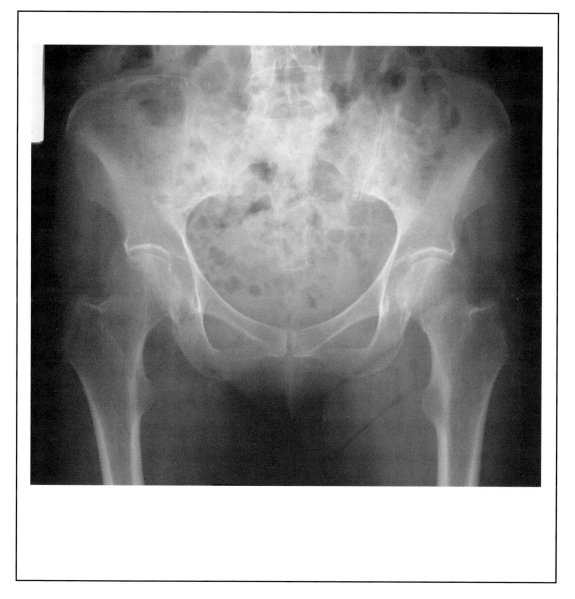

Answer to Case 16

There is a fractured left neck of femur demonstrated by a sclerotic line and step in the cortex.

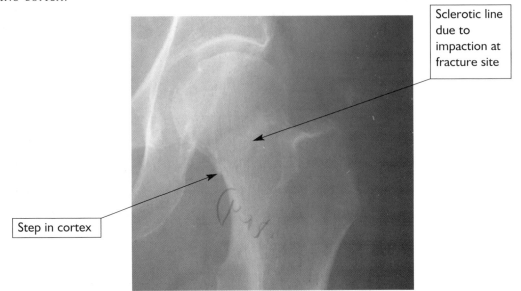

Sclerotic line due to impaction at fracture site

Step in cortex

Femoral neck fractures usually result from a fall and are highly associated with fractures of the distal radius and ulna and proximal humerus in the elderly. There are classically three types of fracture, subcapital being the most common (as in this case). Sometimes the fracture may spiral around the neck, making it difficult to assess which type of fracture of the neck it is. These fractures can be extremely subtle; Shenton's line can be useful in the search for fractured neck of femur. Normally Shenton's line forms a smooth arc as shown on page 71;, steps or breaks in it are indicative of fracture.

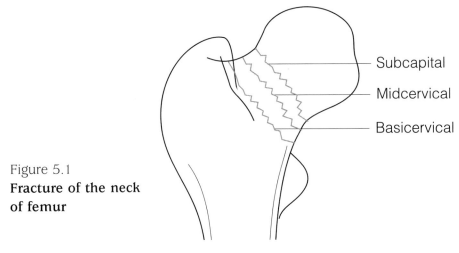

Subcapital

Midcervical

Basicervical

Figure 5.1
Fracture of the neck of femur

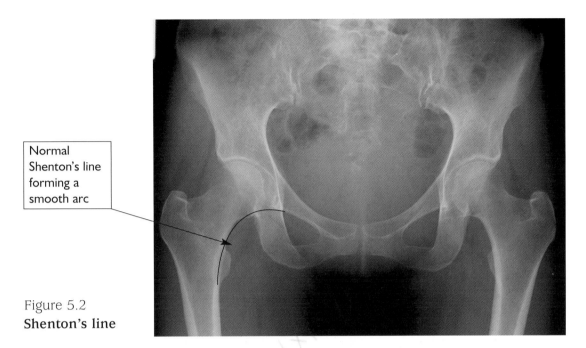

Normal
Shenton's line
forming a
smooth arc

Figure 5.2
Shenton's line

When assessing the pelvic radiograph for fractured neck of femur, look carefully at the trabeculae of the neck of femur. There are two types of trabeculae, compressive and tensile (which have an orientation as demonstrated in Figure 5.3); changes in alignment or steps/breaks in these trabeculae can be the only signs of a subtle fracture of the neck of femur. Other clues to injury may be alterations in the angulation of the neck of femur; there may be varus or valgus angulation, or there may be a foreshortened neck of femur (see Figure 5.4 on page 72). Be careful that ring osteophytes are not mistaken for a sclerotic fracture impaction line.

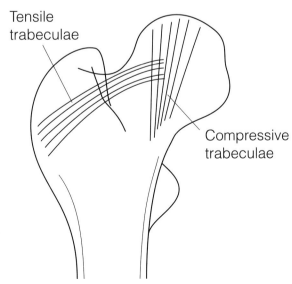

Tensile
trabeculae

Compressive
trabeculae

Figure 5.3
**Trabeculae of the neck
of femur**

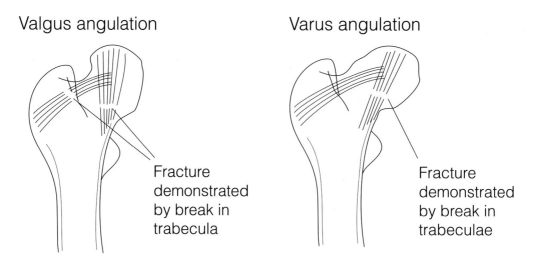

Valgus angulation

Varus angulation

Fracture demonstrated by break in trabecula

Fracture demonstrated by break in trabeculae

Figure 5.4

Fractured necks of femur demonstrated by alterations in trabeculae pattern and aligment of femoral neck

Case 17

Patient has increased pain in hip and is walking with great difficulty.

Describe the radiograph.

Is Shenton's line intact?

What is the name for this?

What disease process causes it?

Which other bones may have a similar appearance?

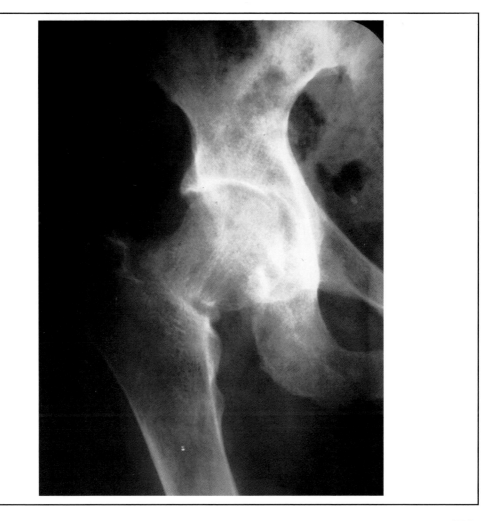

Answer to Case 17

There is a lucent area at the neck of the femur; this appearance is called a Looser's zone, sometimes referred to as a pseudofracture or incomplete fracture. With continued use it can lead to a complete fracture. Looser's zones are caused by osteomalacia; they are incomplete stress fractures which heal with callus lacking in calcium, and are most often seen in the pubic rami, the necks of the femora and humeri and the axillary edge of the scapulae.

Shenton's line in this case is broken and lacks its normal smooth curve.

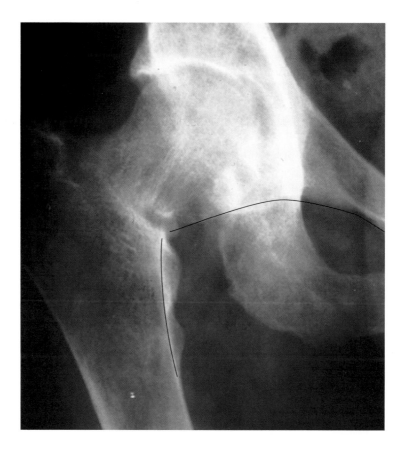

Shenton's line

Osteomalacia is predominantly caused by lack of vitamin D. The people most often affected are the frail elderly and people of South Asian origin (in children it is rickets). Bone is made up of four major components:

- Mineral (mainly calcium and phosphorus)
- Matrix (collagen fibres)
- Osteoclasts
- Osteoblasts.

There is continual bone turnover; when normal bone is formed the collagen fibres are coated with mineral. The strength of the new bone depends on enough mineral covering the collagen matrix. Osteomalacia occurs if mineralisation does not occur properly, resulting in 'soft bones' which may bend and crack. To allow mineralisation to take place the body needs enough minerals, calcium, phosphorus and vitamin D; if not the body develops osteomalacia. However, in Western countries not having enough calcium is not found as a cause of osteomalacia. Certain rare inherited diseases can cause normal kidneys to lose phosphorus, which causes osteomalacia, but the most common cause is lack of vitamin D.

As well as from diet, the body makes its own vitamin D when sunlight falls on the skin; this causes cholesterol in the skin to turn into vitamin D. The body can turn this into a hormone 'cacitriol', the active form of vitamin D, which encourages calcium and phosphorus to be absorbed from the intestine; these form the bone matrix. As the skin becomes thinner with age, less vitamin D is formed, but normally enough is made. But elderly people who are unable to leave the house through ill health, or people who cover their skin for religious reasons, are less likely to receive enough vitamin D by this method and must rely on dietary intake, or vitamin D supplements to prevent osteomalacia.

Case 18

Patient fell on to hip.

Describe the radiograph.

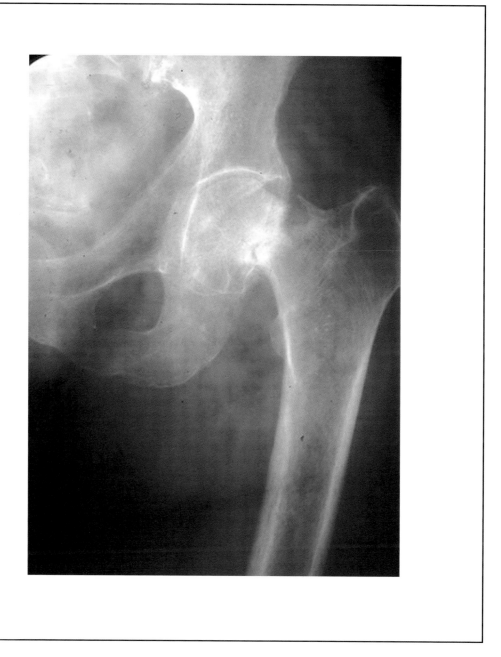

Answer to Case 18

There is a fracture of the neck of femur, demonstrated by a lucent and sclerotic line. The distal part of the fracture has moved proximally. (Remember, always describe movement of the distal part of a fracture.)

Case 19

Patient fell on to hip.

Is there a fracture present?

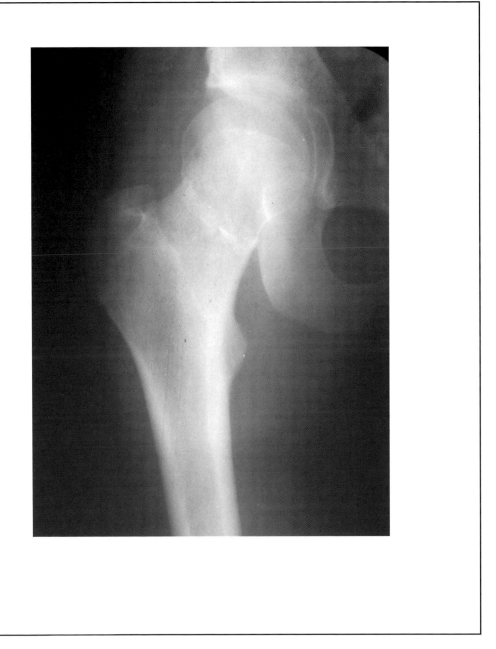

Answer to Case 19

Again there is a fracture of the neck of femur, demonstrated by a sclerotic line and valgus deformity. These are often surgically repaired, by insertion of a hemiarthroplasty (an Austin Moore).

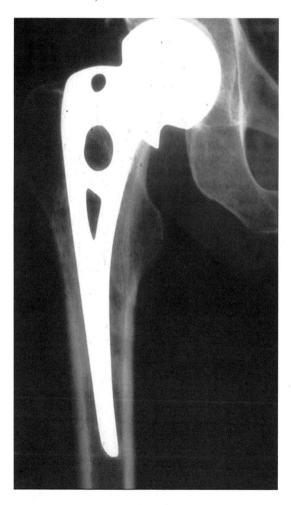

Figure 5.5 **Hemiarthroplasty**

Case 20

Elderly patient fell on to hip.

Describe the radiograph.

What is the name of the fracture?

Can you label the bony anatomy on the lateral radiograph?

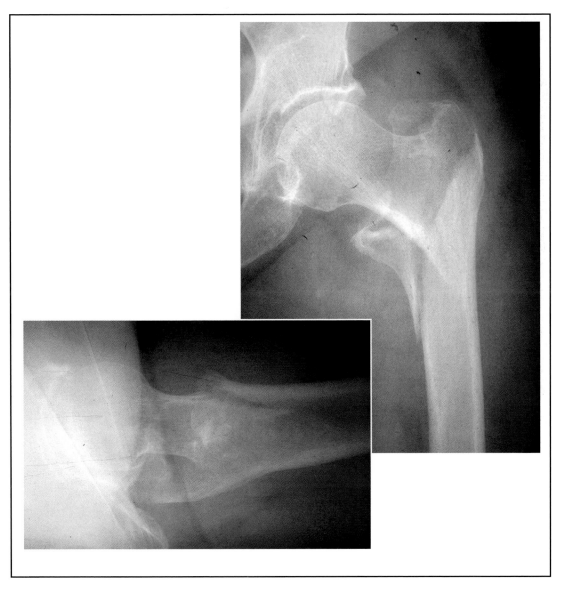

Answer to Case 20

This is an intertrochanteric fracture of the hip with a separate fracture of the lesser trochanter. They tend to occur in an older age group than subcapital fractures of the hip. They can be divided into two-, three- or four-part fractures depending on involvement of the greater and lesser trochanter (see Figure 5.6). The intertrochanteric fracture in this case is a three part, as the lesser trochanter is also fractured.

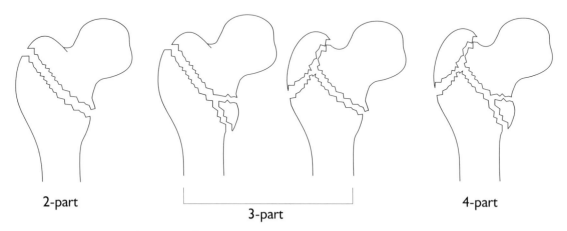

2-part   3-part   4-part

Figure 5.6 **Intertrochanteric fractures**

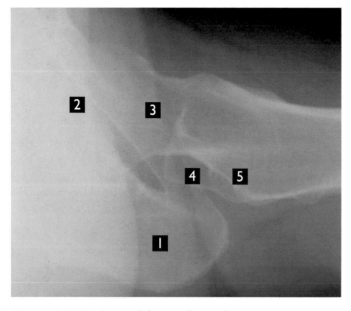

Figure 5.7 **Horizontal beam lateral**

1. Ischial tuberosity
2. Femoral head
3. Femoral neck
4. Greater tuberosity
5. Lesser tuberosity

Case 21

Patient fell down steps.

Review this radiograph first, for an injury, before viewing the lateral radiograph overleaf.

What is the normal orthopaedic procedure following this type of injury?

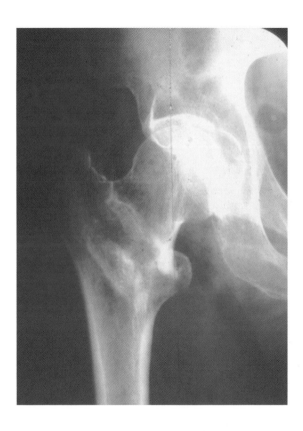

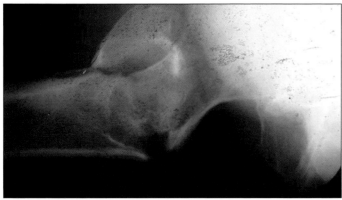

lateral radiograph

Answer to Case 21

The lateral view readily demonstrates that this is a three-part intertrochanteric fracture. The fracture was demonstrated on the anterior posterior view by an intertrochanteric sclerotic area and a step in the cortex. Remember, fractures are demonstrated by a sclerotic or lucent line with a step or break in the cortex (see Sakthivel-Wainford 2006).

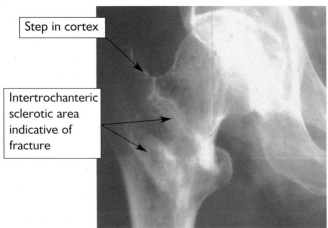

Step in cortex

Intertrochanteric sclerotic area indicative of fracture

Fractures of this type are usually internally fixed with a dynamic hip screw.

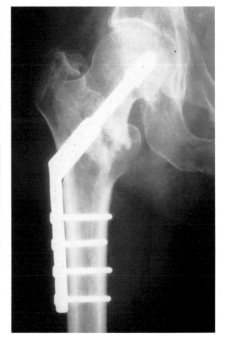

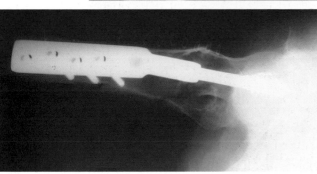

Figure 5.8 **Dynamic hip screw**

84

Case 22

Elderly patient fell, pain in pelvic area, has longstanding painful left hip.

Poor historian, unable to identify where bony tenderness is.

Also, due to patient condition, difficulty obtaining a diagnostic radiograph.

Is there an injury present? What longstanding condition of the hip is demonstrated?

Would another radiographic view be helpful?

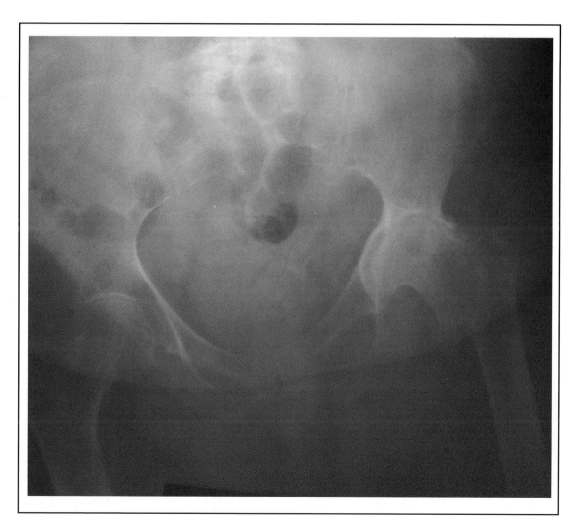

Answer to Case 22

There is an intertrochanteric fracture of the left hip, which is difficult to visualise due to overshadowing soft tissue. The left hip also demonstrates degenerative changes with protusio acetabulum. A lateral radiograph of the left hip is required to assess displacement. The lateral radiograph demonstrates a two-part intertrochanteric fracture.

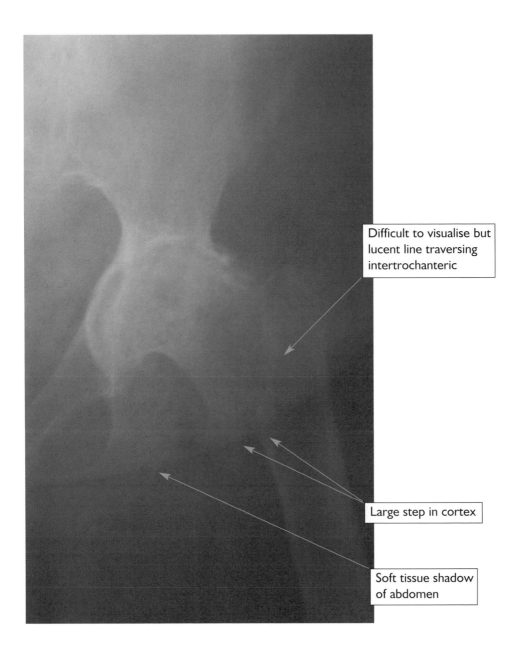

Difficult to visualise but lucent line traversing intertrochanteric

Large step in cortex

Soft tissue shadow of abdomen

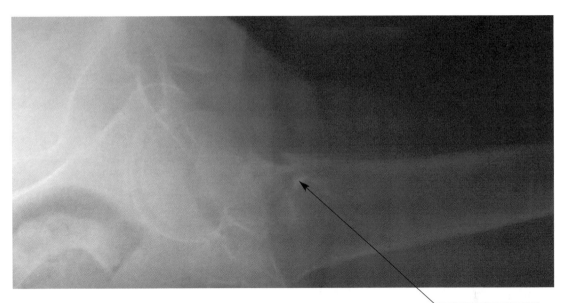

Horizontal beam lateral view

Intertrochanteric
fracture, two-part

Remember, when reviewing the hip for fracture:
- Look for cortical break/step.
- Look for lucent/sclerotic line.
- Check Shenton's line.
- Look at trabeculae pattern.
- Check profile of the femoral neck.
- Compare one side to the other on the pelvis radiograph.
- Consider the diagnostic efficacy of the study.

Case 23

Patient fell in garden.

Describe the radiograph.

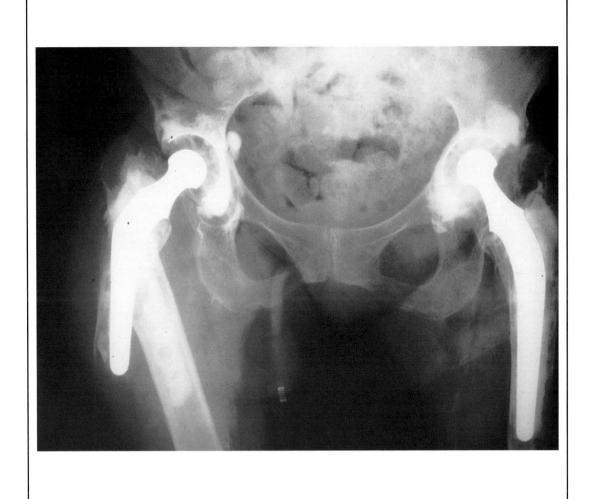

Answer to Case 23

The patient has bilateral hip replacements. There is a fracture of the right femur at the tip of the hip replacement, allowing the distal hip replacement to displace laterally from the femur. There is no dislocation at the hip joint. Several lucent areas are demonstrated in the right femur around the hip replacement; these are indicative of infection or loosening of the replacement.

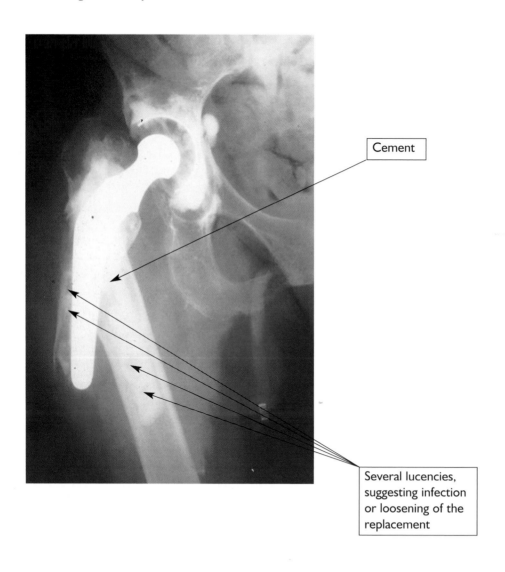

Cement

Several lucencies, suggesting infection or loosening of the replacement

Case 24

Describe the radiographs.

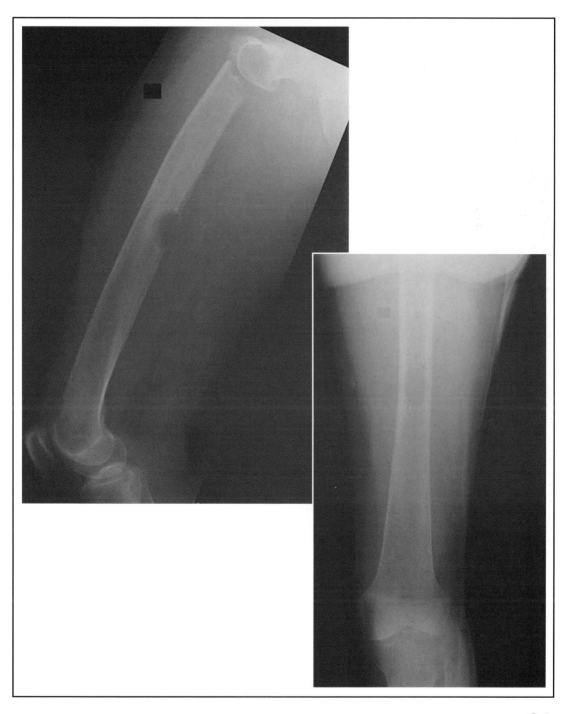

Answer to Case 24

There is a well-defined lucency demonstrated on the anterior posterior radiograph mid-shaft femur, visualised on the lateral radiograph as involving about half the diameter of the shaft and destroying the cortex. The lateral view also demonstrates a pathological fracture of the neck of femur. The mid-shaft lucency was found to be a secondary deposit.

If a pathological fractured neck of femur is present, the orthopaedic surgeon will require radiographs of the whole length of femur prior to surgery to search for further secondaries. Sometimes, if there is a secondary that has not broken the cortex more distal to the neck of femur, the surgeon will inset a full femoral nail as a prophylactic measure.

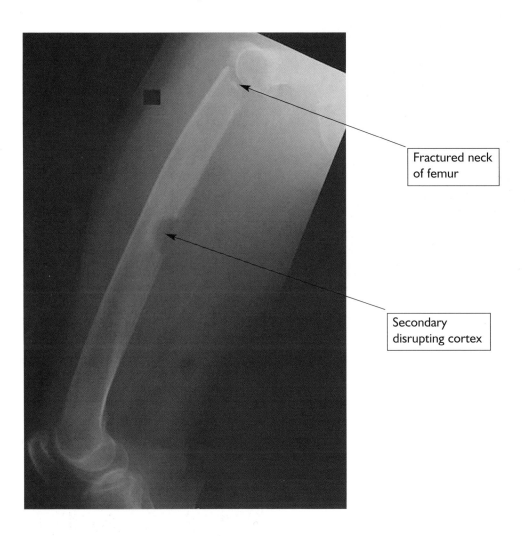

Fractured neck of femur

Secondary disrupting cortex

Case 25

Elderly patient fell on to knee.

Describe the radiographs.

Name the different fractures that occur in the distal femur.

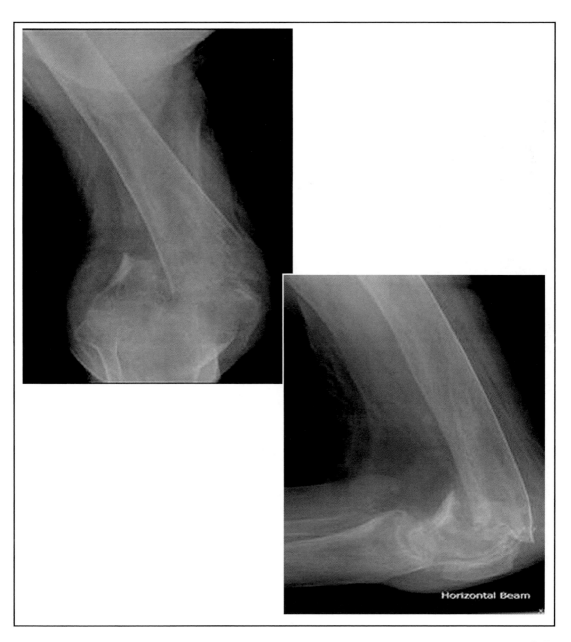

Answer to Case 25

There is a transverse impacted supracondylar fracture of the femur, with dorsal and lateral displacement of distal part. (Remember, when describing fracture displacement to comment on movement of the distal part.) The different fractures of the distal femur are demonstrated in Figure 5.9.

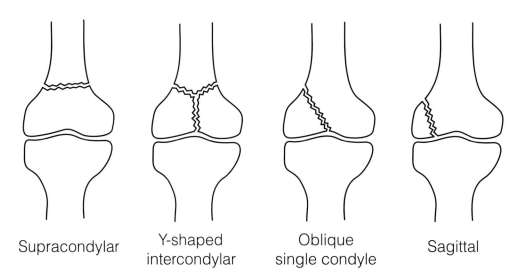

| Supracondylar | Y-shaped intercondylar | Oblique single condyle | Sagittal |

Figure 5.9 **Fractures of the distal femur**

Case 26

It was only possible to obtain one radiograph on this patient, following a fall.

Describe the radiograph.

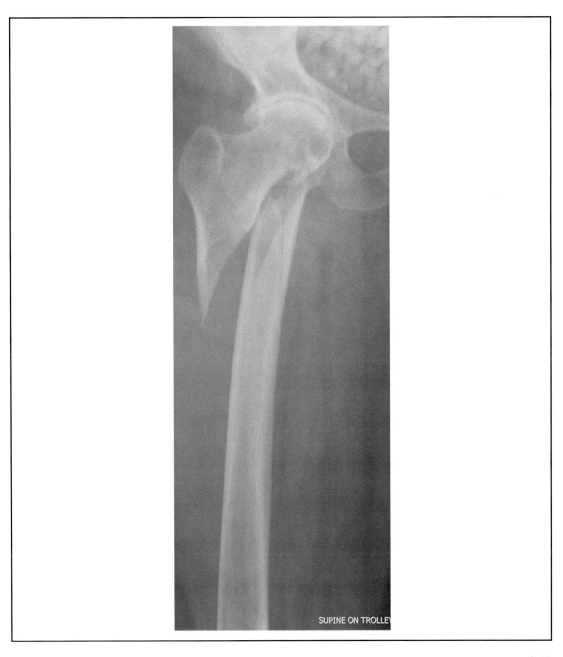

SUPINE ON TROLLEY

Answer to Case 26

There is an oblique subtrochanteric fracture (i.e. below the lesser and greater trochanters), with medial and proximal movement of the distal part. A second longitudinal fracture line can be seen starting from the main fracture, passing down the femur.

Case 27

Patient fell out of bed on two occasions, several weeks apart.

Now unable to weight bear, with painful left hip, which is externally rotated and foreshortened.

Describe the radiographs.

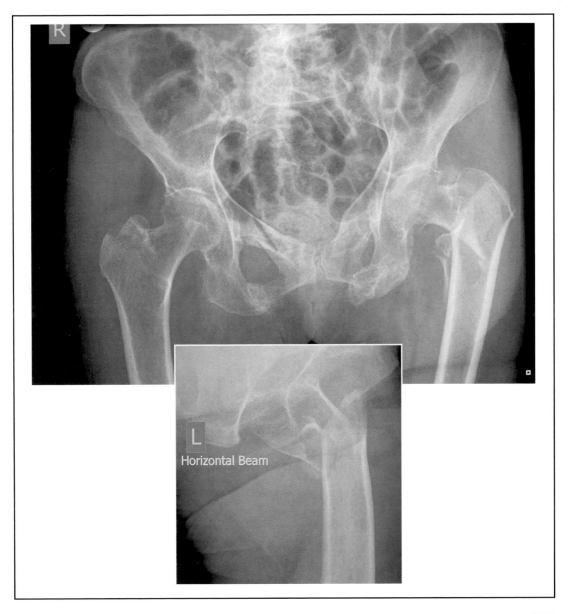

Answer to Case 27

There are many fractures present, some old, some new. There are old fractures of the left superior and inferior pubic rami (fracture lines no longer readily visible). There is a four-part intertrochanteric fracture of the left hip, resulting in clinical presentation of foreshortened and externally rotated hip. The right side of the pelvis demonstrates a fracture of the greater trochanter, superior and inferior pubic rami. The lateral radiograph of the left hip demonstrates the anterior and proximal displacement of the distal femur.

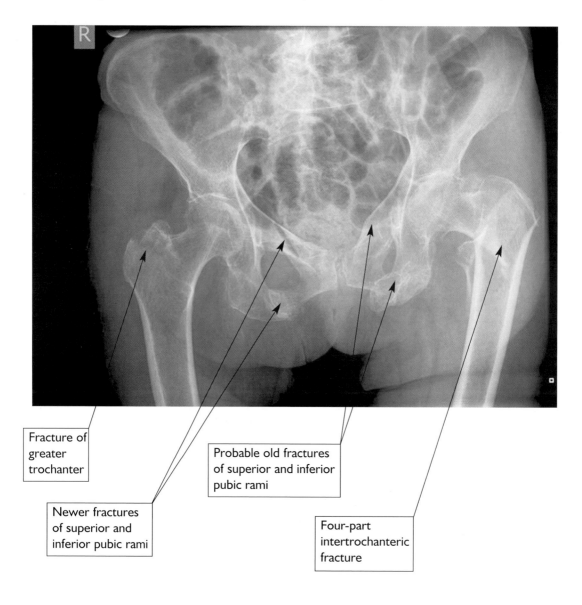

Fracture of greater trochanter

Newer fractures of superior and inferior pubic rami

Probable old fractures of superior and inferior pubic rami

Four-part intertrochanteric fracture

Case 28

Patient had previous surgery to the right hip following a fall.

Patient has fallen again in the garden, now pain proximal femur and difficulty weight bearing.

Is there an injury present?

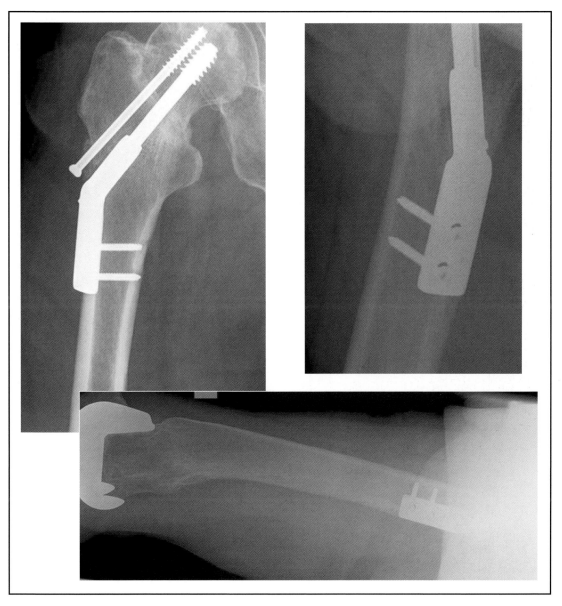

Answer to Case 28

The patient has a cannulated hip screw, and a dynamic hip screw, plus a knee replacement. Just below the dynamic hip screw is a subtle lucent line on the anterior posterior view, close to the second pin of the dynamic hip screw, but no break in the cortex. The lateral hip and femur views again demonstrate the subtle lucent line, the lateral hip view demonstrating a break in the cortex – hence although subtle a definite fracture. (Remember from book one fractures are demonstrated by lucent/sclerotic line associated with a step/break in the cortex.)

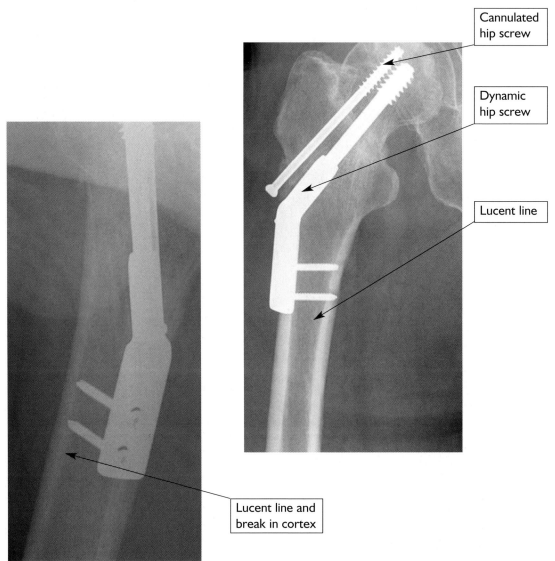

Cannulated hip screw

Dynamic hip screw

Lucent line

Lucent line and break in cortex

Case 29

Patient fell, injuring femur.

Describe the radiographs.

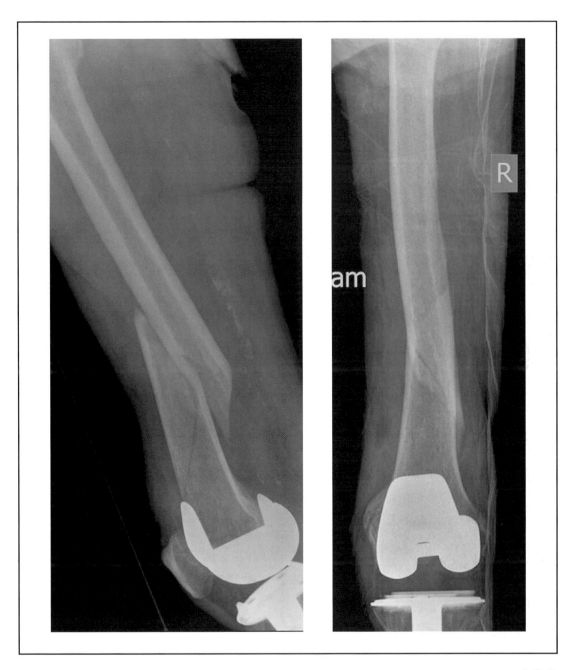

Answer to Case 29

There is a spiral fracture of the distal femur superior to the knee replacement. There is foreshortening of the femur and anterior displacement of the distal femur.

Case 30

This is an old case. Patient had fractured their hip and had internal fixation. They then fell again several weeks later and had increased pain and reduced mobility. Can you see any injury?

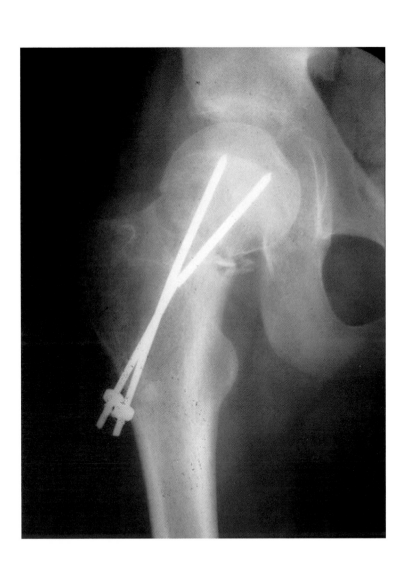

Answer to Case 30

There is an old fracture of neck of femur with 2 pins inserted.
There is a break in one of the pins, maybe caused by the second fall.

Break in pin

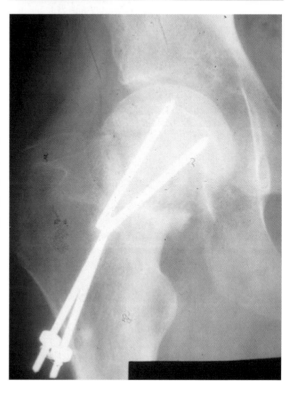

The patient was referred to orthopaedics and follow up films at intervals were taken. The next one shows the break in the pin more clearly; the last one demonstrates removal of the distal broken part of the pins and collapse of the femoral head.

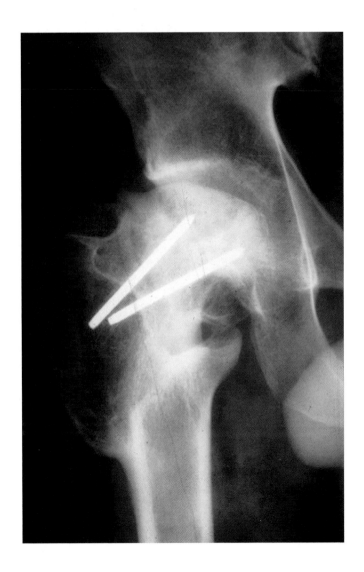

6.

Cervical spine trauma

Case 31

Patient was front seat passenger in a road traffic accident, now has pain in neck.

Is there an injury?

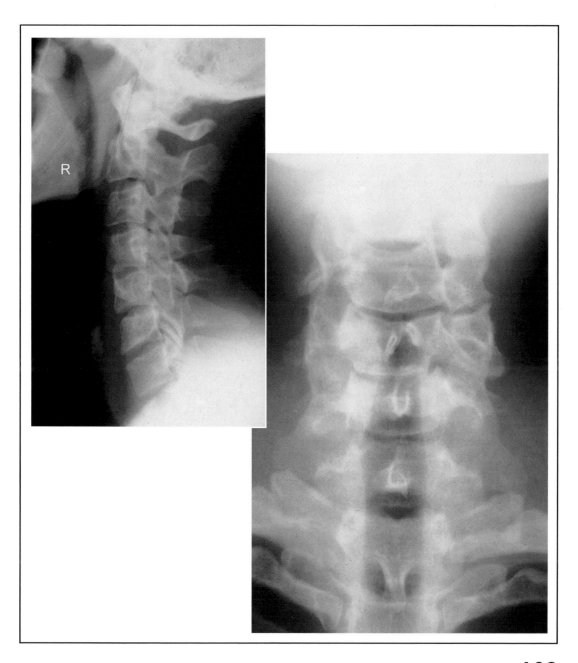

Answer to Case 31

The initial radiographs were assessed by a radiographer practitioner, who then asked advice of a consultant radiologist. The lateral view is not a true lateral view. Consequently there is some overlapping of the facet joints, making interpretation difficult, although there is no soft tissue sign of injury. The antero posterior view demonstrates a bifid cervical spine at cervical vertebra 5, and some irregularity of the lateral masses at this level. The radiologist suggested a repeat lateral radiograph, the opposite lateral view to the original.

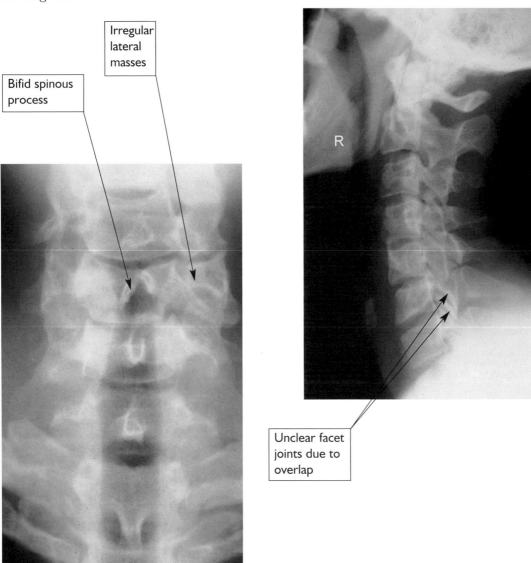

Irregular lateral masses

Bifid spinous process

R

Unclear facet joints due to overlap

The repeat lateral demonstrates the facet joints (like tiles on a roof), and vertebrae clearly. On this radiograph there appears to be no sign of trauma. The patient was sent for a CT scan of the cervical spine, which demonstrated no injury. It was concluded that there was no trauma to the cervical spine, and the appearances of the initial radiographs were due to congenital abnormalities.

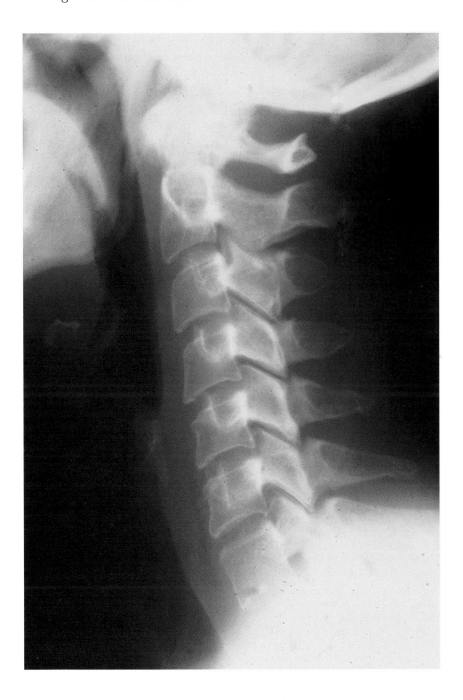

Case 32

Patient fell down a flight of stairs, trauma radiographs were carried out in the resuscitation room.

Does this radiograph demonstrate an abnormality?

What are the names of the five lines that can be used in assessing the lateral trauma radiograph?

Are any further radiographs required?

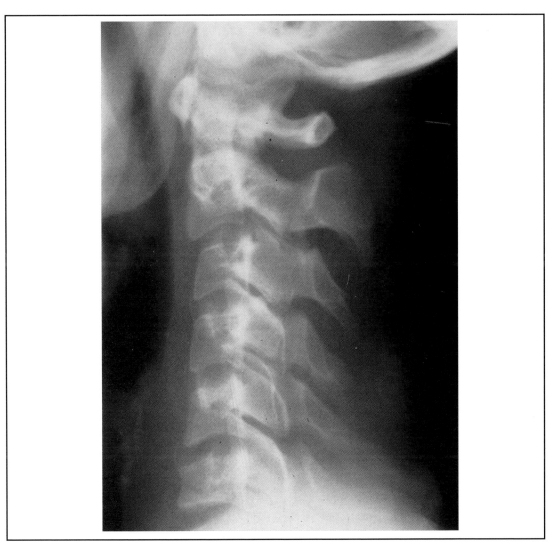

Answer to Case 32

There is a step in the anterior and posterior spinal lines at cervical vertebra two. In addition, the joint space between cervical vertebrae 2 and 3 is no longer parallel; it is increased posteriorly. On closer inspection a lucent line can be visualised through the posterior elements of cervical vertebra 2. This is called bilateral traumatic spondylolisthesis of cervical vertebra 2, commonly known as hangman's fracture (following judicial hanging).

These fractures are usually the result of hyperextension of the head on the neck, but may occur following hyperflexion and compression. The injury occurs when hyperextension of the head, through the pedicles on to the apophyseal joints, causes a fracture anterior to the inferior facet of cervical vertebra 2 – the weak point in the chain. The lateral radiograph demonstrates the injury best.

The five lines used when reviewing lateral radiographs are: anterior spinal line, posterior spinal line, spinolaminar line, posterior pillar line and spinous line (see Chapter 3 for their description and radiographic demonstration). Sometimes with a 'hangman's fracture' the fracture line is difficult to see but the clues to injury are loss of alignment of anterior and posterior spinal lines and widened intervertebral space.

To complete a cervical spine radiographic investigation, ideally anterior posterior and odontoid peg views should be carried out, but the initial lateral radiograph should always demonstrate from cervical vertebra 1 to the joint space of cervical vertebra 7 dorsal vertebra 1, even if this requires a swimmer's view in the resuscitation room. The initial lateral radiograph does not demonstrate the lower cervical spine and there does appear to be some loss of alignment at cervical vertebra 6/7 with widening of the intervertebral distance, indicative of trauma. Remember, if you see one fracture on a cervical vertebra radiograph always look for another.

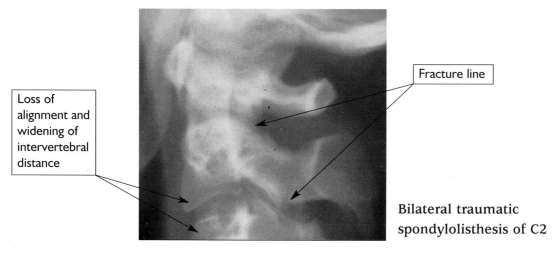

Fracture line

Loss of alignment and widening of intervertebral distance

Bilateral traumatic spondylolisthesis of C2

Case 33

Patient was involved in a road traffic accident.

Describe the radiograph.

Comment on the different types of 'hangman's fracture'.

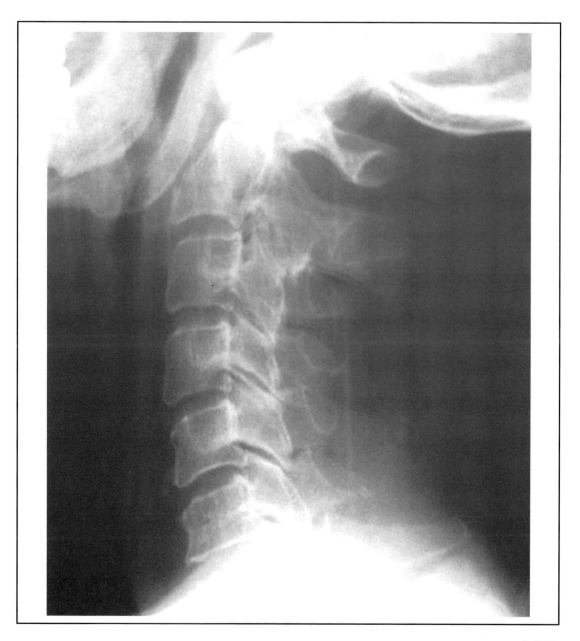

Answer to Case 33

There is transverse fracture of cervical vertebra 2 extending horizontally into the posterior elements.

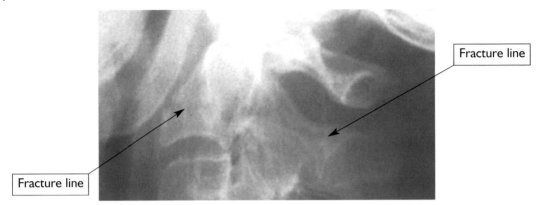

Hangman's fractures have been classified by Effendi into different types (see Figure 6.1), depending on whether they are undisplaced (type I), they have an extension or flexion tilt or there is subluxation of the facet joints (type II), or type III with dislocated facet joints. The hangman's fracture in Case 32 (see pages 105–106) is a type II flexion tilt.

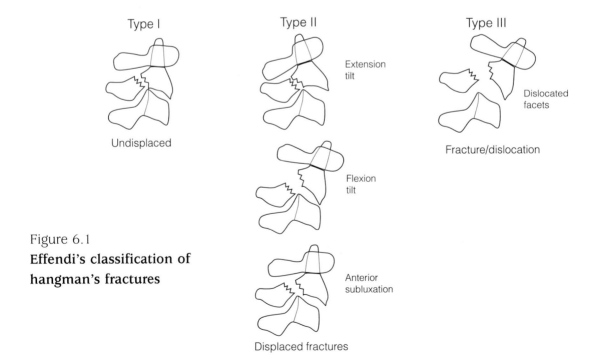

Figure 6.1
Effendi's classification of hangman's fractures

Case 34

Patient fell off horse.

Before looking at radiograph over the page, assess this radiograph for signs of trauma.

Then classify the injury over the page.

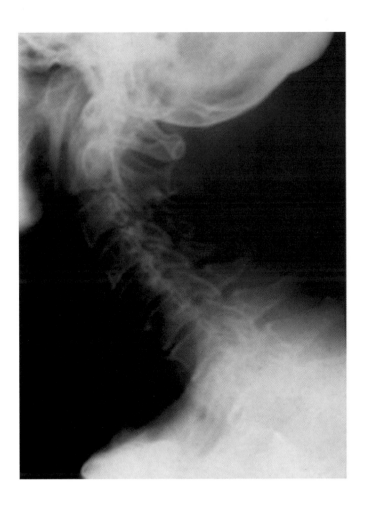

Answer to Case 34

The radiograph on page 109 is not a true lateral radiograph. However, there is widening of the cervical vertebra 2/3 level anterior, with a slight offset of the anterior spinal line, which as mentioned in Case 32 can be indicative of a hangman's fracture. A lateral flexion radiograph was taken with assistance from the orthopaedic surgeon; this clearly demonstrates a fracture of the posterior elements. It is an Effendi type II, extension tilt with possible subluxation of the facet joints.

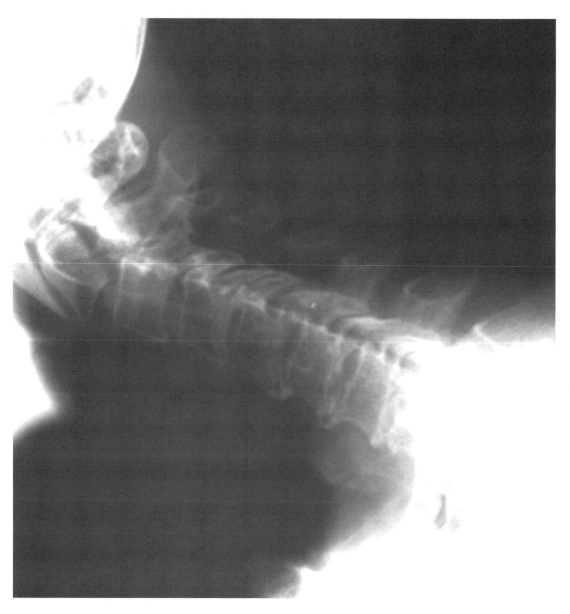

Case 35

Patient fell while climbing.

Describe the collimated radiograph of the area of interest.

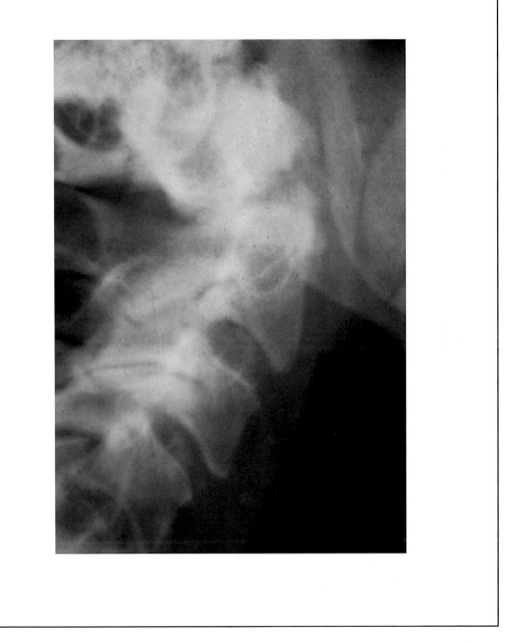

Answer to Case 35

There is a transverse fracture of the odontoid peg; also a fracture of the posterior elements of cervical vertebra 1.

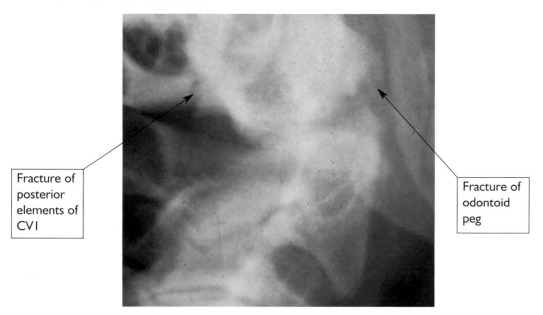

Fracture of posterior elements of CVI

Fracture of odontoid peg

Most odontoid peg fractures occur through the base of the peg and are demonstrated on the open mouth view. Be careful of composite shadows overlying the odontoid peg on the open mouth view, especially the occipital bone or teeth, which may be mistaken for a fracture (commonly known as the 'mach' effect). Soft tissue swelling is normally present in patients with odontoid fracture and can be visualised on the lateral radiograph.

Andersen classified odontoid fractures into three types: type I involving tip of odontoid, type II involving base of odontoid and type III involving base of odontoid and some of the body of cervical vertebra 2 (see Figure 6.2).

Type I   Type II   Type III

Figure 6.2
Andersen
classification
of odontoid
fractures

Case 36

Patient was involved in a road traffic accident, now has pain in neck.

Describe the radiograph.

What is an os odontoideum?

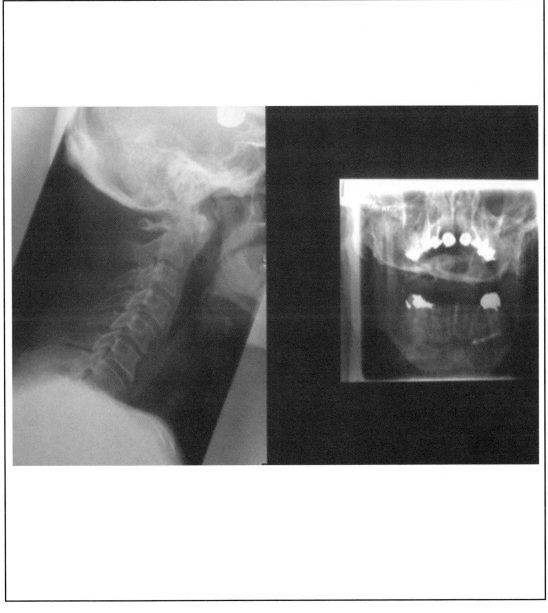

Answer to Case 36

There is a fracture of the base of the odontoid process. The os odontoideum is a result of overgrowth of the os terminale and a hypoplastic odontoid. Congenital abnormalities of the odontoid can make interpretation of trauma difficult. The normal ossification centre of the tip of the odontoid process sometimes fails to fuse, resulting in the os terminalae (see Figure 6.3).

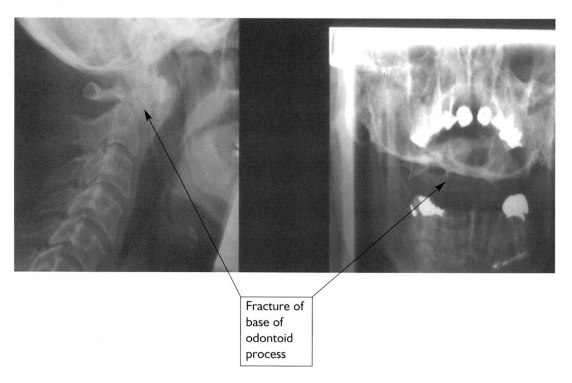

Fracture of base of odontoid process

Figure 6.3 **Os terminale variants**

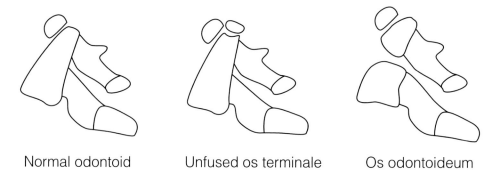

Normal odontoid   Unfused os terminale   Os odontoideum

Case 37

Patient diving into sea from a height, injured neck.

Describe the radiograph.

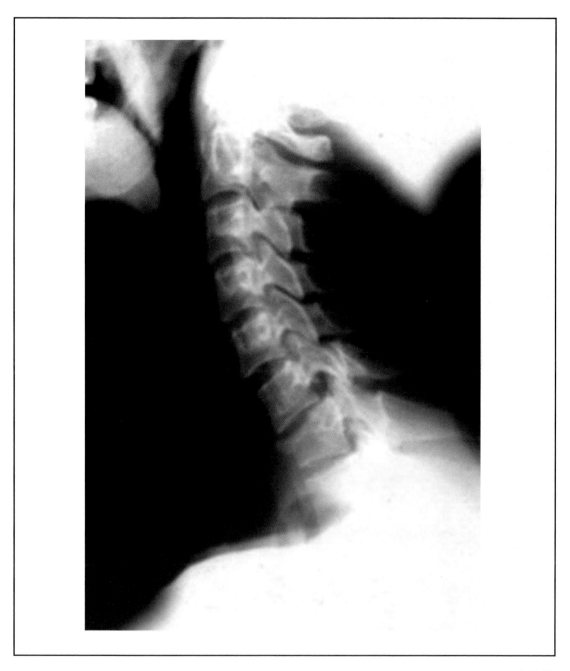

Answer to Case 37

There is a bilateral interfacetal subluxation and crush fracture of cervical vertebra 6.

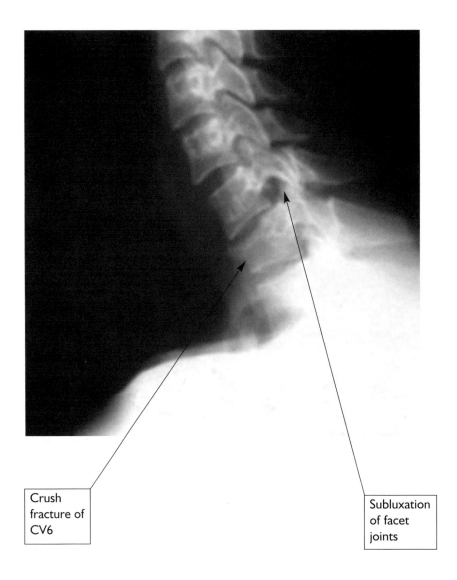

Crush
fracture of
CV6

Subluxation
of facet
joints

Case 38

Patient was shovelling wet soil.

Now has pain in neck.

Describe the radiograph.

What is the common name for this injury?

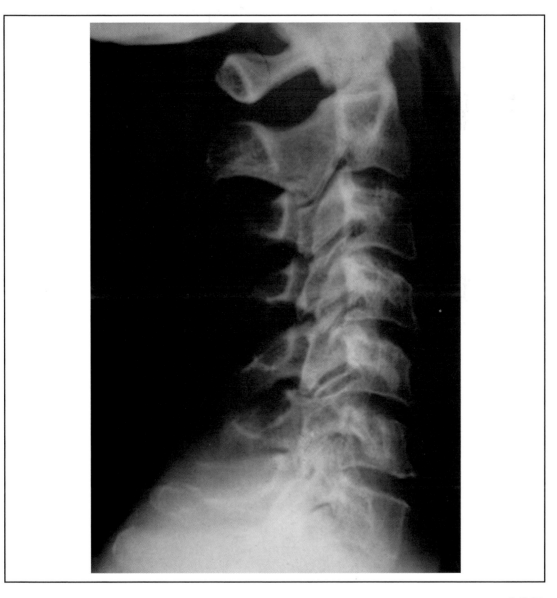

Answer to Case 38

There is a fracture of the spinous process of cervical vertebra 7, often called 'Clay shoveller's fracture'. It is named after road workers, who, when shovelling wet, heavy clay, put so much strain on the ligaments attached to the spinous process of cervical vertebra 7 as to avulse the tip of the spinous process.

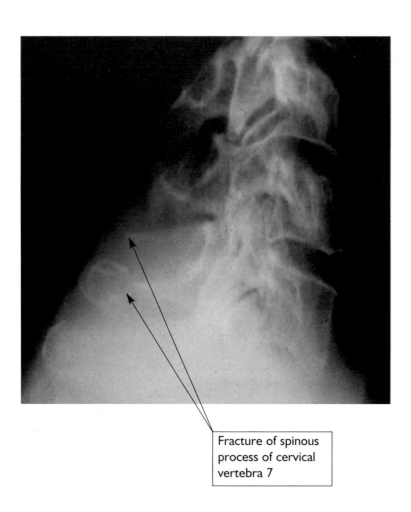

Fracture of spinous
process of cervical
vertebra 7

Case 39

Describe the signs of trauma demonstrated on this collimated radiograph.

What is the name for this type of injury?

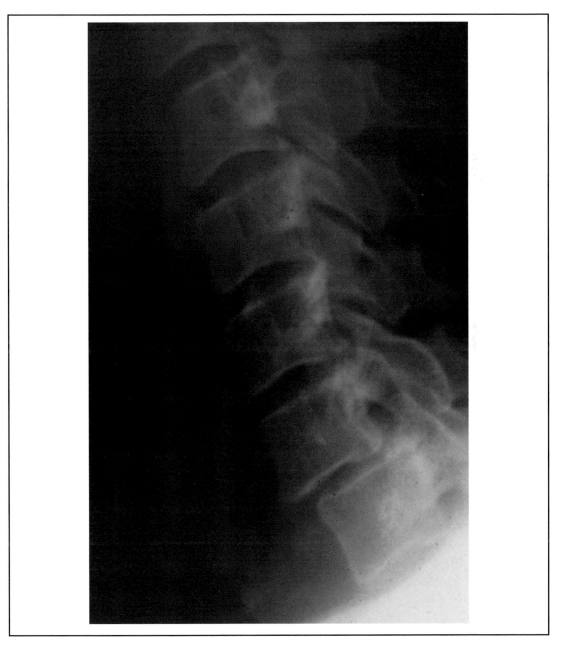

Answer to Case 39

There is a step in the anterior and posterior spinal lines at cervical vertebrae 6/7. There is also some soft tissue swelling (see pages 29–30), and misalignment of the facet joints at this level. Cervical vertebra 6 is placed approximately 25% anterior to cervical vertebra 7 – this is indicative of a unilateral anterior facet dislocation. The most common mechanism of injury for a unilateral facet dislocation is a flexion injury. The anterior posterior view will demonstrate sudden offset of the spinous processes at the level of the facet dislocation.

As well as 25% anterior displacement, the lateral view may demonstrate a loss of the normal square appearance of the vertebral body as it rotates; this rotation may continue to give a 'bow tie' appearance. The lateral view may also demonstrate narrowing between the spinolaminar line and the cortex of the facet.

Figure 6.4

Anterior posterior view of cervical spine with unilateral facet dislocation

Sudden offset of spinous process

Narrowing between spinolaminar line and cortex of facet

Figure 6.5

Lateral view of unilateral facet dislocation

"Bowtie" appearance

About 25% displacement

Case 40

Patient fell while climbing up a cliff, now has pain in neck.

Describe the radiograph.

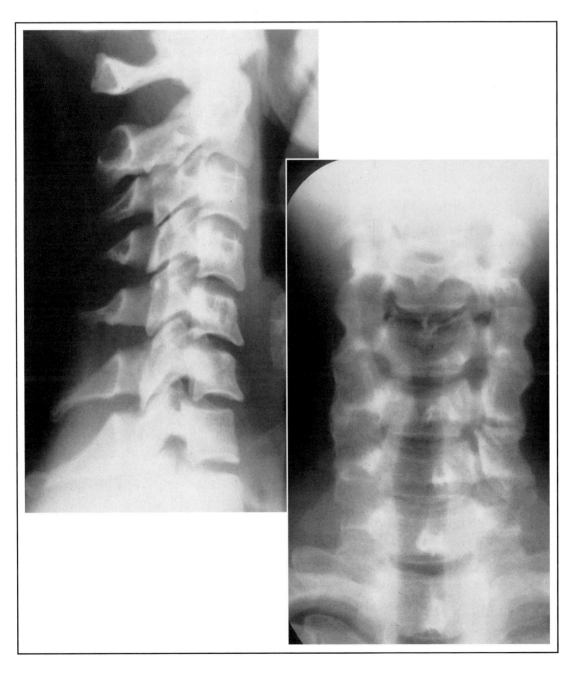

Answer to Case 40

The lateral radiograph appears similar to the previous case with anterior displacement of one vertebra to another by about 25%; in this case anterior displacement at cervical vertebrae 5/6. The anterior posterior view, however, demonstrates a fracture of the lateral pillar at this level. This is a pillar type fracture. The patient hyperextended their neck while falling but also rotated their head to the left (to see where they were falling), compressing and fracturing the left lateral pillar, as demonstrated on the radiograph. There is also some subluxation of the facet joints at this level.

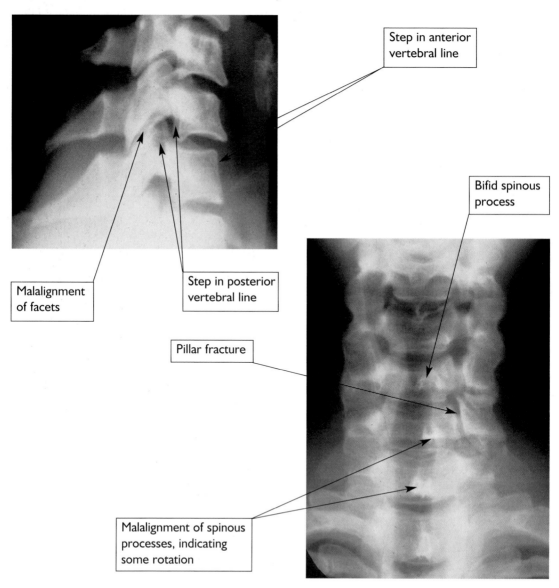

Step in anterior vertebral line

Bifid spinous process

Malalignment of facets

Step in posterior vertebral line

Pillar fracture

Malalignment of spinous processes, indicating some rotation

Case 41

Patient was involved in a road traffic incident.

Describe the radiographs.

What is the common name for this type of injury?

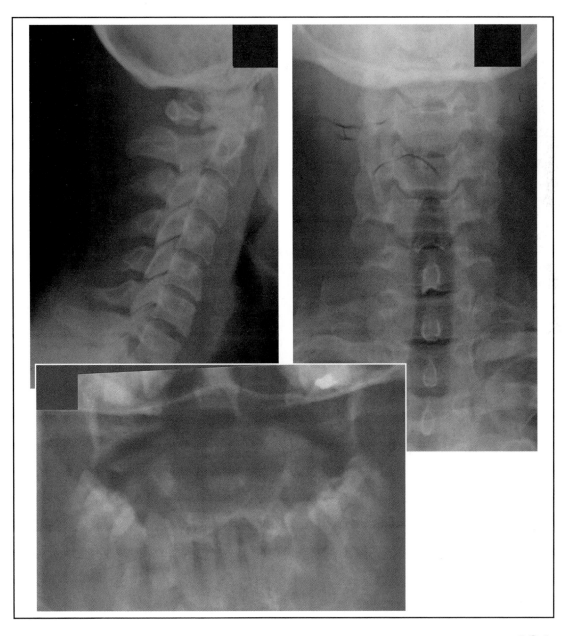

Answer to Case 41

The lateral view demonstrates a fracture of the posterior part of cervical vertebra 1; the open mouth view demonstrates malalignment of axis and atlas, and widening of the space between odontoid process and cervical vertebra 1. This represents a burst fracture of cervical vertebra 1, commonly called a Jefferson's fracture. Notice also the increase in soft tissue shadow anterior to CV 1.

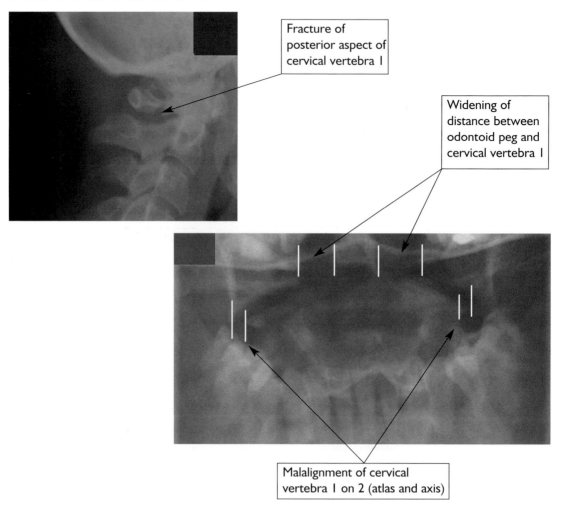

Fracture of posterior aspect of cervical vertebra 1

Widening of distance between odontoid peg and cervical vertebra 1

Malalignment of cervical vertebra 1 on 2 (atlas and axis)

The open mouth view demonstrates the degree of lateral mass spreading, occasionally offsetting may be seen only on one side. Stability is implied when total offset of the two sides on the open mouth view is less than 7mm; greater disruption than this implies instability and disruption of the transverse ligament.

Case 42

Patient fell down several steps, now has pain in neck.

Is there an injury demonstrated on this radiograph?

Describe the radiograph.

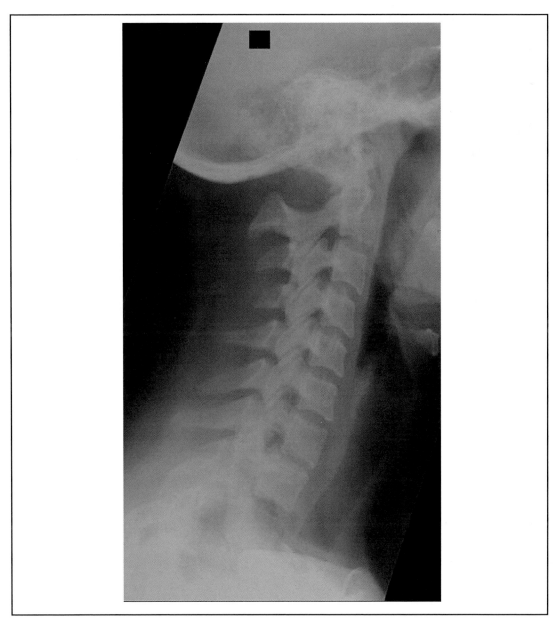

Answer to Case 42

There is no injury demonstrated on this radiograph. However, there is congenital abnormality: no posterior part of cervical vertebra 1.

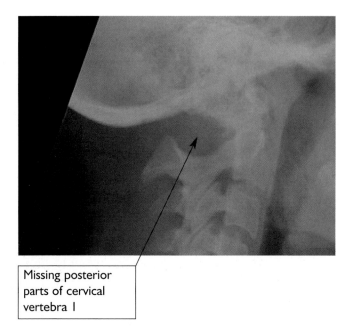

Missing posterior parts of cervical vertebra 1

Case 41

Patient was involved in a road traffic incident.

Describe the radiographs.

What is the common name for this type of injury?

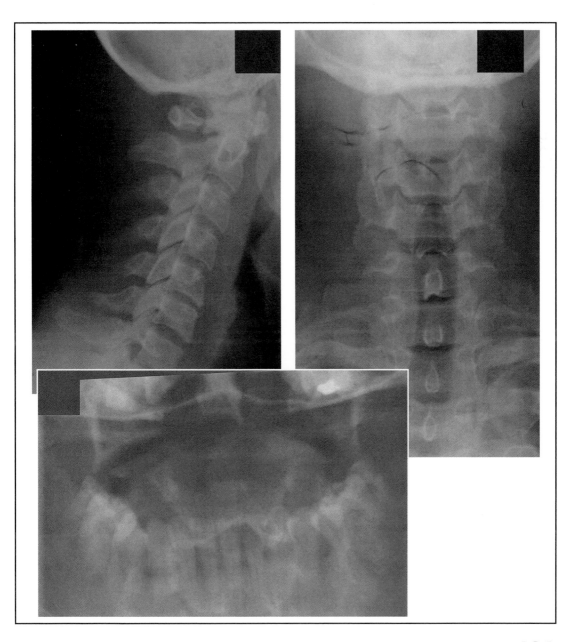

Answer to Case 41

The lateral view demonstrates a fracture of the posterior part of cervical vertebra 1; the open mouth view demonstrates malalignment of axis and atlas, and widening of the space between odontoid process and cervical vertebra 1. This represents a burst fracture of cervical vertebra 1, commonly called a Jefferson's fracture. Notice also the increase in soft tissue shadow anterior to CV 1.

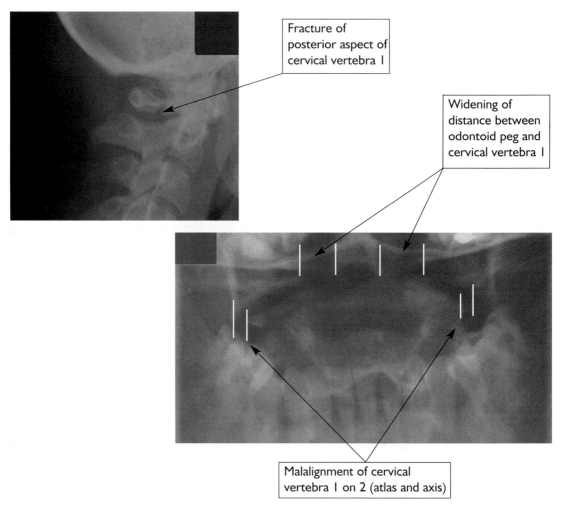

Fracture of posterior aspect of cervical vertebra 1

Widening of distance between odontoid peg and cervical vertebra 1

Malalignment of cervical vertebra 1 on 2 (atlas and axis)

The open mouth view demonstrates the degree of lateral mass spreading, occasionally offsetting may be seen only on one side. Stability is implied when total offset of the two sides on the open mouth view is less than 7mm; greater disruption than this implies instability and disruption of the transverse ligament.

Case 42

Patient fell down several steps, now has pain in neck.

Is there an injury demonstrated on this radiograph?

Describe the radiograph.

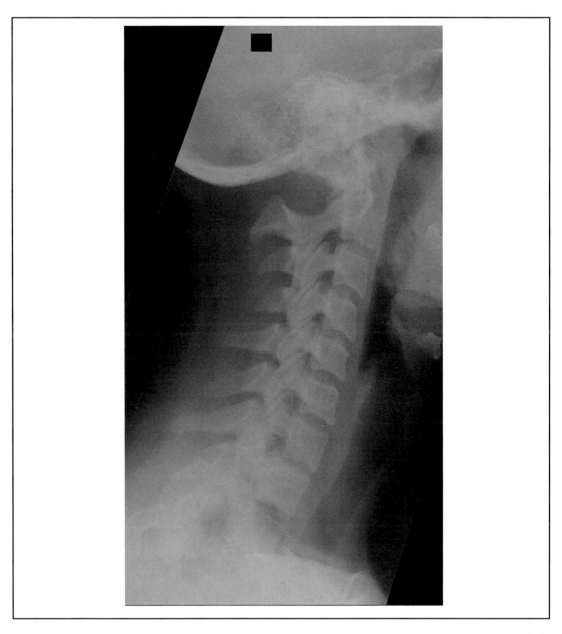

Answer to Case 42

There is no injury demonstrated on this radiograph. However, there is congenital abnormality: no posterior part of cervical vertebra 1.

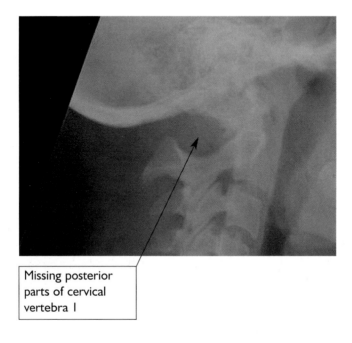

Missing posterior parts of cervical vertebra 1

Case 41

Patient was involved in a road traffic incident.

Describe the radiographs.

What is the common name for this type of injury?

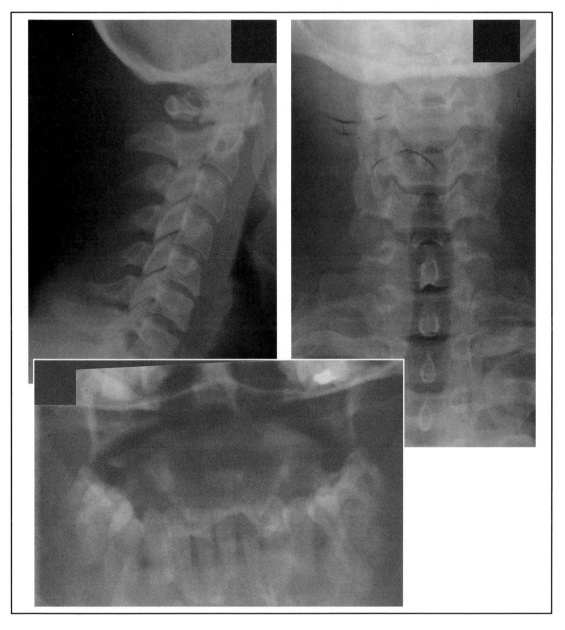

Answer to Case 41

The lateral view demonstrates a fracture of the posterior part of cervical vertebra 1; the open mouth view demonstrates malalignment of axis and atlas, and widening of the space between odontoid process and cervical vertebra 1. This represents a burst fracture of cervical vertebra 1, commonly called a Jefferson's fracture. Notice also the increase in soft tissue shadow anterior to CV 1.

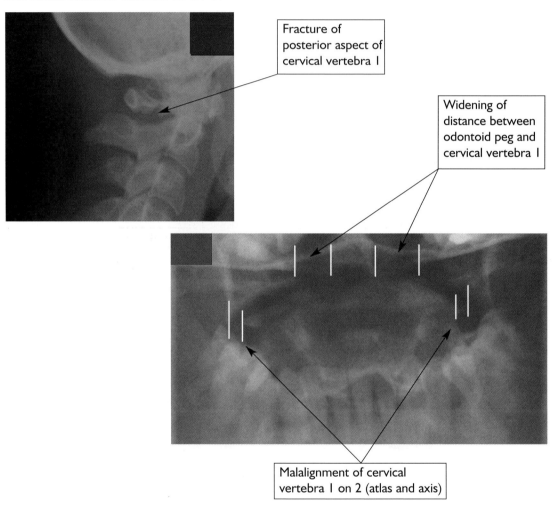

Fracture of posterior aspect of cervical vertebra 1

Widening of distance between odontoid peg and cervical vertebra 1

Malalignment of cervical vertebra 1 on 2 (atlas and axis)

The open mouth view demonstrates the degree of lateral mass spreading, occasionally offsetting may be seen only on one side. Stability is implied when total offset of the two sides on the open mouth view is less than 7mm; greater disruption than this implies instability and disruption of the transverse ligament.

Case 42

Patient fell down several steps, now has pain in neck.

Is there an injury demonstrated on this radiograph?

Describe the radiograph.

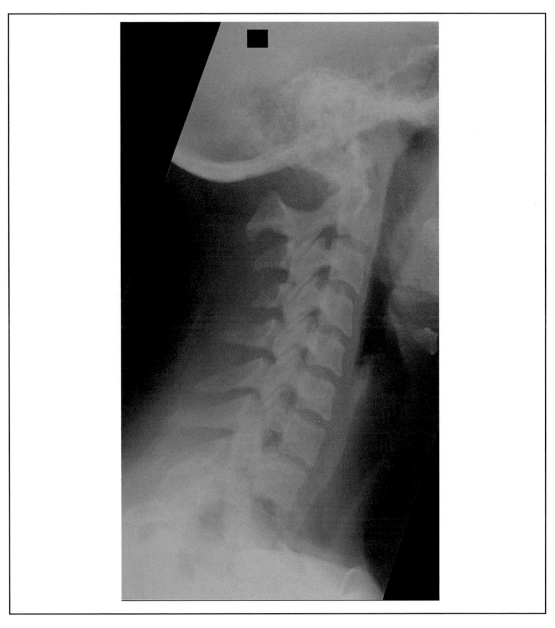

Answer to Case 42

There is no injury demonstrated on this radiograph. However, there is congenital abnormality: no posterior part of cervical vertebra 1.

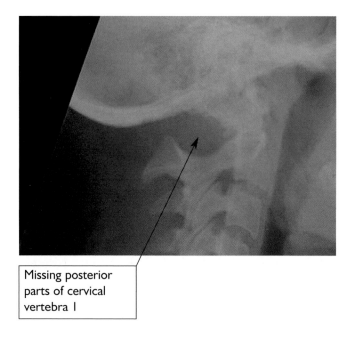

Missing posterior parts of cervical vertebra 1

Case 43

Patient was involved in a road traffic accident.

Describe the injury.

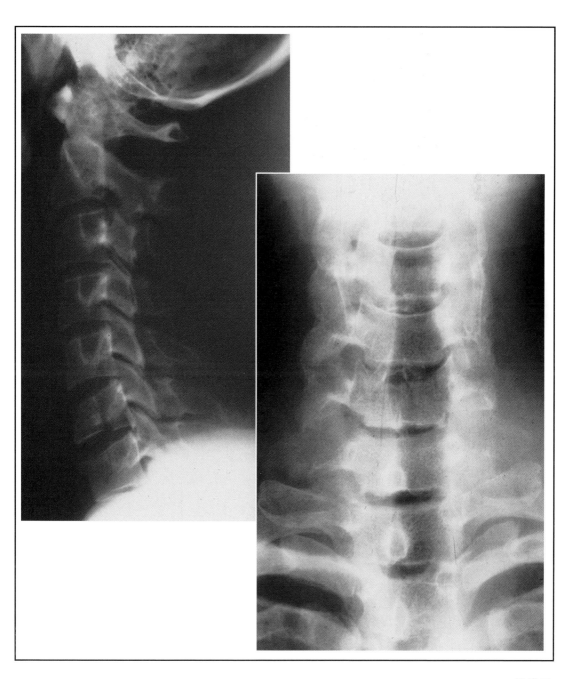

Answer to Case 43

There is a burst fracture of cervical vertebra 6, demonstrated by a lucent line, break in cortex and a flattened vertebra, as it has burst.

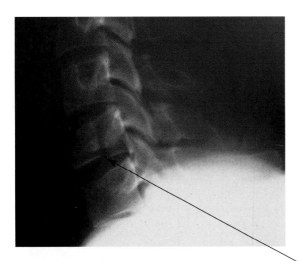

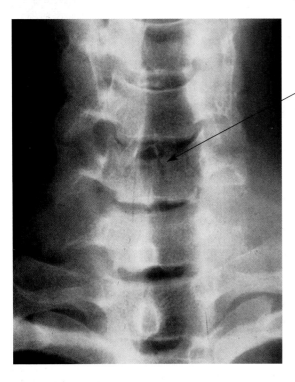

Burst fracture
of cervical
vertebra 6

Case 44

Patient fell from a height into shallow water.

Describe the radiographs.

Is there an injury?

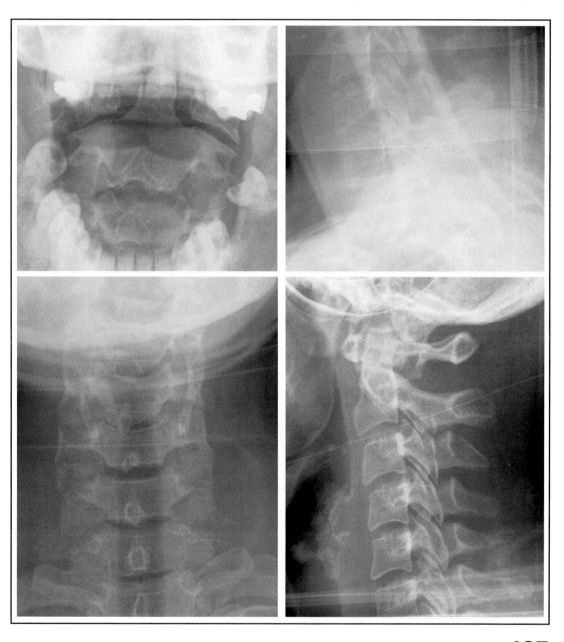

Answer to Case 44

There is a bursting fracture of cervical vertebra 1, resulting in malalignment with cervical vertebra 2 (a Jefferson's fracture). This is visualised on the open mouth radiograph.

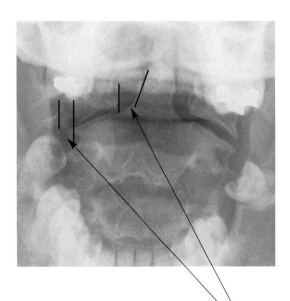

Malalignment of CVI/CV2 indicative of a Jefferson's fracture

Case 45

Unknown male hit by a car.

Lateral cervical spine taken as part of a trauma series in the resuscitation room.

What is shown on this radiograph that should not be seen?

Is there suspicion of an injury?

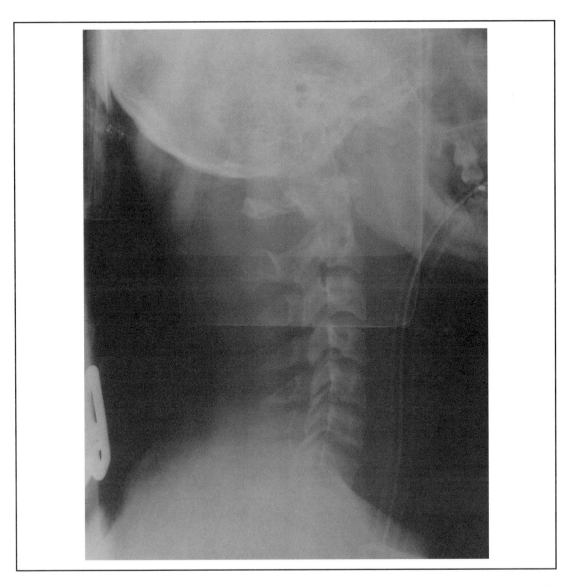

Answer to Case 45

Someone is holding the patient's head; hands are shown on the radiograph. This should not be seen. If it is essential for someone to hold the patient then lead gloves should be worn. Close to one of the fingers there is a probable fracture of the posterior aspect of cervical vertebra 1. This lateral should have been repeated along with an open mouth view, as there is a high suspicion of a Jefferson's fracture from this one radiograph. Unfortunately these radiographs were not able to be performed due to patient's rapidly worsening condition.

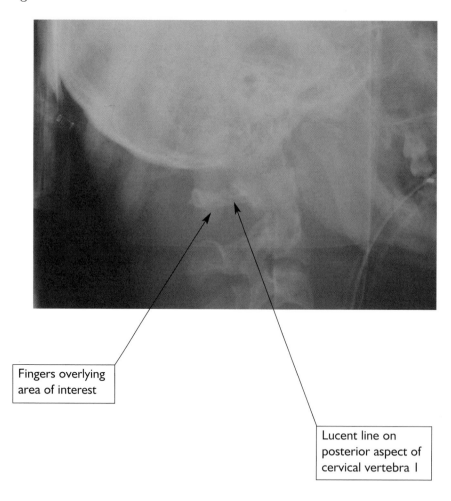

Fingers overlying area of interest

Lucent line on posterior aspect of cervical vertebra 1

7.

Dorsal and lumbar spine trauma

Case 46

Patient was involved in a road traffic accident, now has pain in back.

Describe the radiographs.

How common are injuries of this area?

What soft tissue signs are indicative of fracture of the dorsal spine?

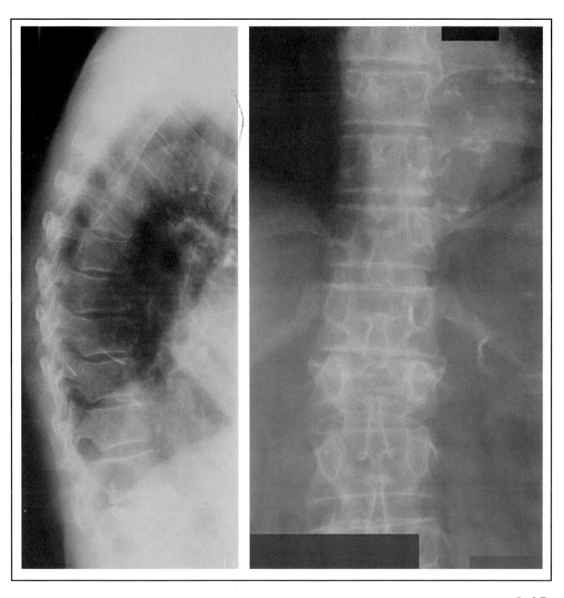

Answer to Case 46

There is a wedge fracture of lumbar vertebra 1. The anterior posterior view demonstrates an increased interpedicular distance compared with the other vertebrae, loss of vertebra height and ill-defined inferior and superior cortices of the vertebral body. The lateral radiograph demonstrates a wedged vertebra below the diaphragm (although not well demonstrated on this radiograph).

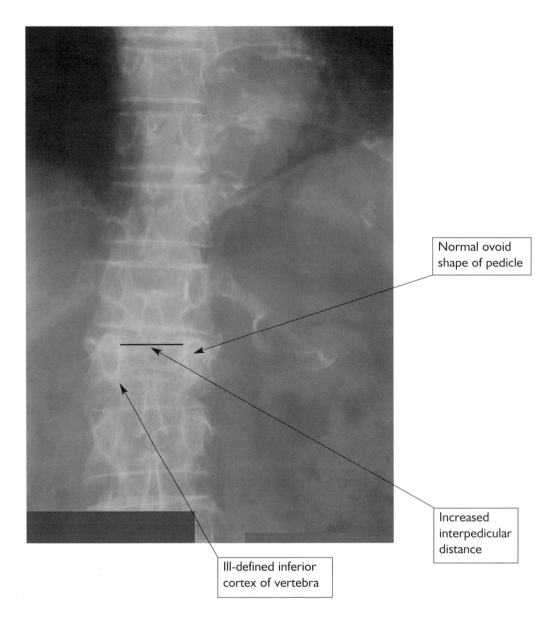

Normal ovoid shape of pedicle

Increased interpedicular distance

Ill-defined inferior cortex of vertebra

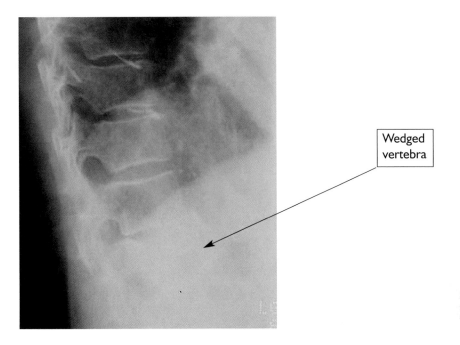

Wedged vertebra

In adults 60 to 70 % of fractures occur at thoracic vertebra 12, lumbar vertebrae 1, 2, with 90 % of all fractures of the dorso-lumbar spine being demonstrated between thoracic vertebra 11 and lumbar vertebra 4. Fractures of the upper and mid-thoracic spine are uncommon in adults, but are often associated with children, particularly at thoracic vertebrae 4/5 level.

On the antero-posterior radiograph of the dorsal spine one should check the paraspinal lines; widening of the paraspinal lines implies haemorrhage, which may be due to spinal injury. Also, remember to check for increased interpedicular distance, and buckling of the lateral cortices of the vertebral body.

Fracture of the thoraco-lumbar spine can generally be grouped into several mechanisms of injury: compression fractures, burst fractures, distraction fractures (Chance fractures and other lapseat belt injuries), and fracture dislocation injuries.

In 1983 Denis introduced the concept of a three-column spine classification system for acute injuries to the thoraco-lumbar spine.
- The anterior column includes the anterior two-thirds of the annulus fibrosus and vertebral body, and anterior longitudinal ligament.
- The middle column includes the posterior longitudinal ligament, the posterior third of the vertebral body and the annulus fibrosus.
- The posterior column involves the posterior ligament complex, which includes the supraspinous and infraspinous ligaments, the capsule of the intervertebral joints and the ligamentum flavum.

145

The theory is that one-column fractures are stable, and two-column fractures may be stable or unstable depending on extent of injury, whereas three-column fractures are unstable.

This case demonstrates a compression fracture, often resulting from anterior or lateral flexion. It results in a failure of the anterior column, the middle column remaining intact and acting like a hinge; hence it is likely to be stable.

Case 47

Patient had fallen on several occasions, now has pain in lower back.

Describe the radiographs.

What is the name for this appearance?

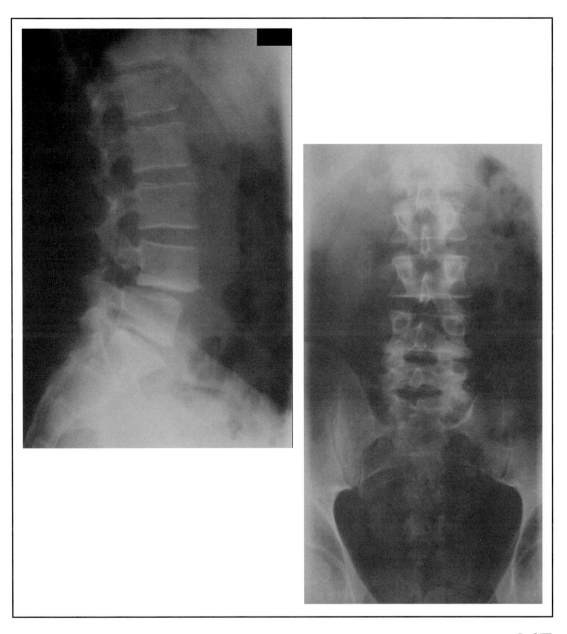

Answer to Case 47

There is a fracture through the pars interarticularis of lumbar vertebra 4, resulting in an offset of lumbar vertebra 4 on 5 – this is called spondylolisthesis. Spondylolisthesis is a term introduced by Killian in 1854 to describe a ventral slipping of all or part of one vertebra on a stationary vertebra below. In a grade 1 spondylolisthesis the offset between the two vertebrae involved is less than 25% (measured against the distal vertebra involved in the offset), measured by the length of the end plate of lumbar vertebra 5 in this case. A grade 2 spondylolisthesis is offset more than 25% but less than 50%; a grade 3 is offset more than 50% (see Figure 7.1). For the vertebral slip to occur, the spondylosis is bilateral, resulting in the vertebral body in the more cephalad position slipping forward on the more caudal body. Not all cases of spondylolisthesis are symptomatic, although if severe it can cause neuroforaminal stenosis and can impinge on the nerve roots of the spinal canal.

Spondylolysis is a break or defect in the pars interarticularis portion of the lamina; this spinal abnormality may not be caused by trauma. Some say it may be congenital, others post traumatic; some believe it is a stress-related injury.

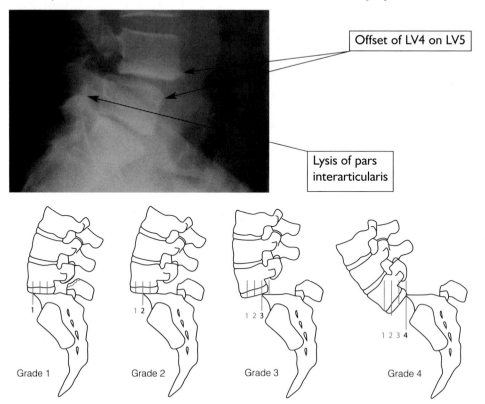

Offset of LV4 on LV5

Lysis of pars interarticularis

Grade 1   Grade 2   Grade 3   Grade 4

Figure 7.1 **Grading of spondylolisthesis**

148

Case 48

Patient attended Accident and Emergency following a fall.

Patient has longstanding lower back pain, now feels worse.

Describe the radiographs.

Are there any other radiographic views that will assist in demonstrating this condition?

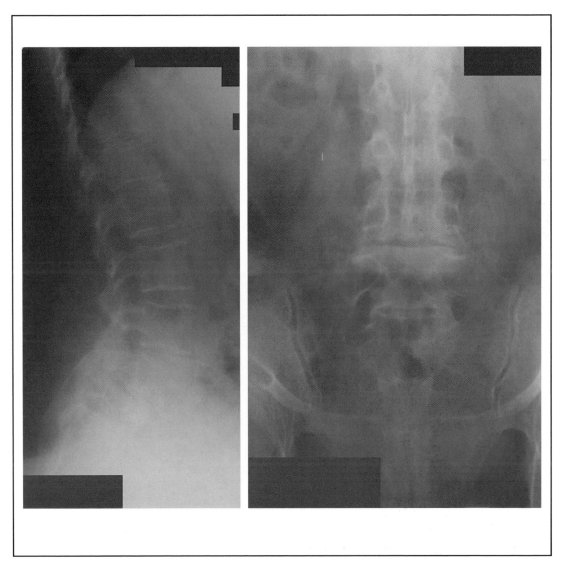

Answer to Case 48

There is a grade 1 spondylolisthesis of lumbar vertebra 5, which is probably longstanding: there is no new fracture. Oblique views can be helpful in demonstrating this abnormality, depending on the protocols of the department. Oblique views demonstrate the interfacetal joints well, and the pars interarticularis (area of the defect). Both oblique views are normally carried out. The appearance of the vertebra body on the oblique radiograph was likened to a Scottie dog by Lachepelle, the neck of the Scottie dog being the pars interarticularis.

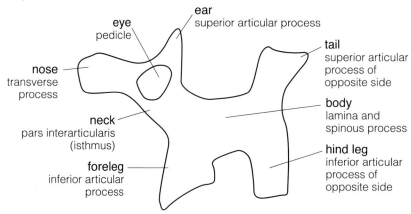

Figure 7.2

The Scottie dog as described by Lachepele, as viewed on oblique lumbar vertebra radiographs

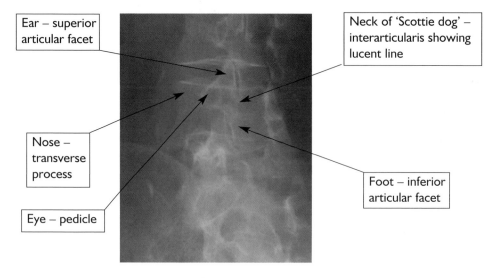

Figure 7.3 **Oblique view of the lumbar spine**

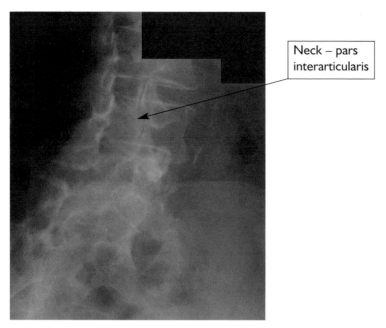

Neck – pars interarticularis

Figure 7.3a **Oblique view of the lumbar spine**

A radiograph coned to lumbar vertebra 5/sacral vertebra 1 can also be helpful in demonstrating this defect. This coned radiograph is more frequently obtained in radiology departments than the oblique radiographs.

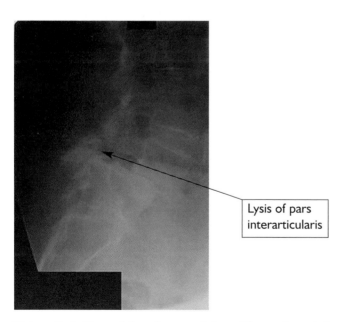

Lysis of pars interarticularis

Figure 7.4 **Coned lumbar vertebra 5/sacral vertebra 1**

Sometimes the ventral slip of one vertebra on another is caused by a lysis of the pars interarticularis (a break in the neck of the Scottie dog), or degenerative changes of the pars interarticularis (a narrowing of the Scottie dog's neck). The first is a true spondylolisthesis, the latter a pseudospondylolisthesis. With a spondylolisthesis, there is a step in the normal continuation of the spinous processes (see Figure 7.5); with a true spondylolisthesis this step of the spinous process is above the level of the vertebra slip; with a pseudospondylolisthesis, the step of the spinous process is below the level of the vertebra slip.

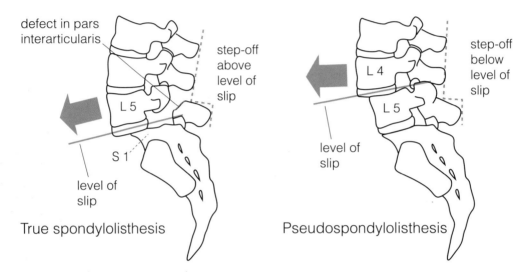

Figure 7.5 **Spinous process signs**

Case 49

Patient fell from scaffolding, now has acute pain in lumbar spine.

Describe the radiographs.

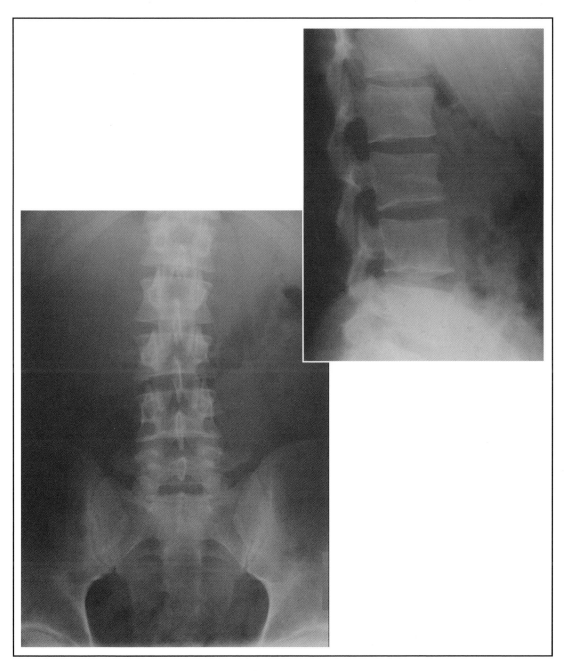

Answer to Case 49

The antero-posterior view demonstrates a slight curvature of the spine, concave to the left. Sometimes following trauma, or in acute pain, the muscles can contract, resulting in a curvature of the spine on the antero-posterior radiograph. The lateral view demonstrates a wedging of lumbar vertebrae 3 and 2, with horizontal sclerotic lines in both vertebra bodies (more pronounced in lumbar vertebra 3), indicative of compressed fractures of both vertebrae.

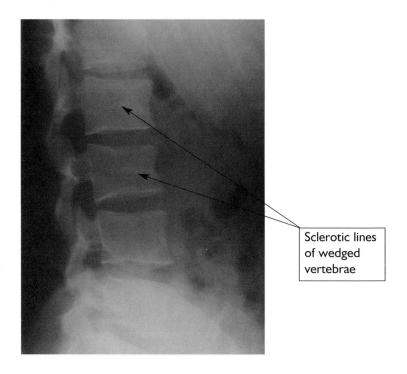

Sclerotic lines
of wedged
vertebrae

Case 50

Patient fell down a flight of stairs, now has pain in lumbar and dorsal spine.

Describe the radiographs on this page and pages 156 and 157.

What is the difference between a compressed fracture and a burst fracture?

How are the columns of the spine affected in each?

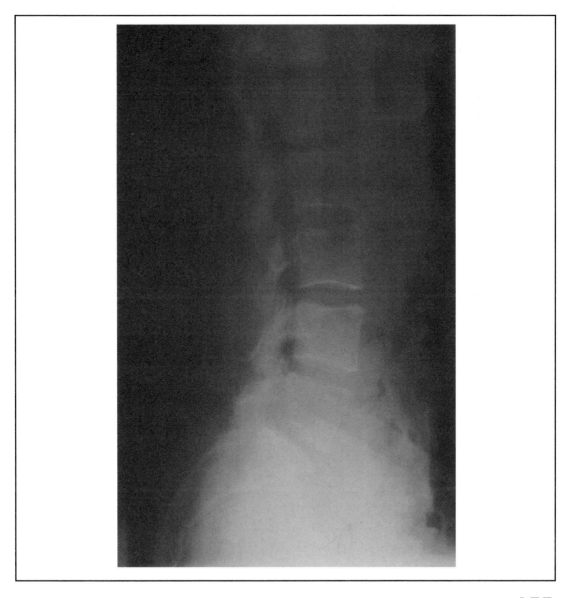

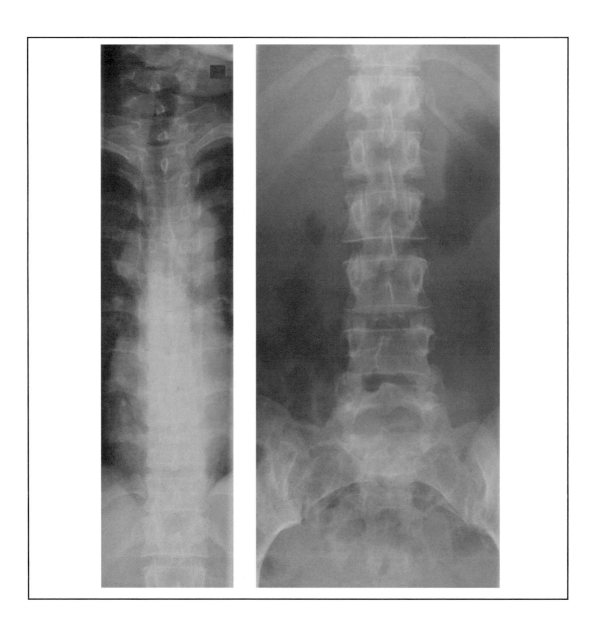

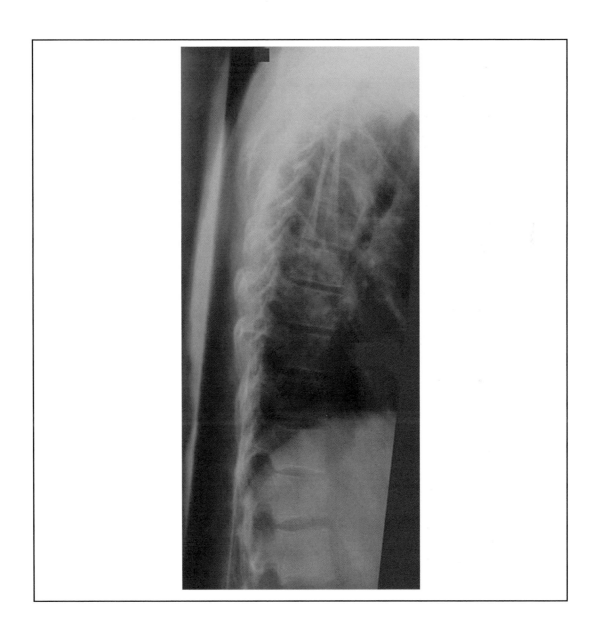

Answer to Case 50

There appears to be a compressed (wedge) fracture of dorsal vertebra 12. Notice the buckling of the anterior superior border of the vertebra and increased width of the vertebra on the lateral view, especially posteriorly.

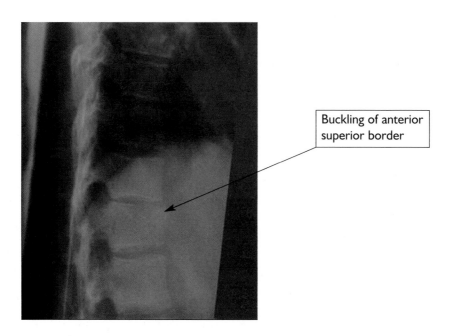

Buckling of anterior superior border

A compression fracture usually results from anterior or lateral flexion, and results in a failure of the anterior column; the middle column normally appears intact. A wedge appearance of the vertebra is often demonstrated on the lateral radiograph.

A burst fracture results from a failure of the anterior and middle columns, following axial compression, sometimes associated with rotation or flexion. The antero-posterior radiograph normally demonstrates a vertical fracture of the vertebra with increase in interpedicular distance. The lateral radiograph demonstrates fracture of the posterior part of the vertebral body, resulting in a decrease in height of that part of the bone. This often results in comminution, with fragments being pushed into the spinal canal. CT is required to assess the full extent of the injury.

This case demonstrates a compressed fracture, with the posterior part of the fracture appearing to involve the spinal canal. CT is required to assess involvement.

Case 51

Patient was involved in a road traffic accident.

Describe the radiographs.

Which columns are affected?

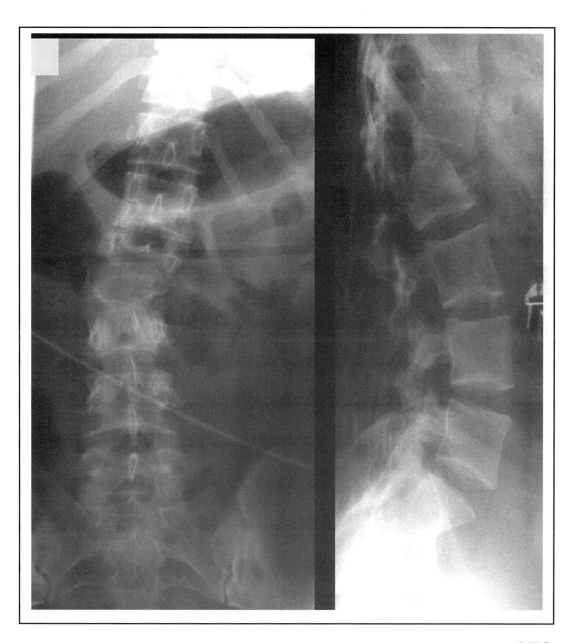

Answer to Case 51

This is a fracture dislocation involving lumbar vertebrae 1 and 2. It will involve all three columns (anterior, middle and posterior), and consequently is very unstable. The antero-posterior view demonstrates fracture of lumbar vertebra 2 with angulation and displacement; on this view lumbar vertebra 1 appears intact. The lateral view demonstrates posterior angulation of lumbar vertebra 2 and what appears to be a separated fragment from the vertebra anteriorly.

Fracture dislocations can result from many different mechanisms; the four main types are flexion rotation, posterior shear, anterior shear and flexion distraction (see Figure 7.6).

- Flexion rotation disrupts the posterior and middle columns, and possibly the anterior column. It is demonstrated on the lateral radiograph by anterior wedging. The lateral radiograph will also demonstrate subluxation or dislocation, with an increase in interspinous distance. If the dislocation occurs at the level of the disc the posterior wall of the vertebra may be intact.
- Shear type fracture involves all three columns, including the anterior longitudinal ligament. The posterior shear variant is demonstrated by forward displacement of the spinal segment on the vertebra below at the level of shear; but the posterior elements are normally fractured at several levels. In anterior shear, the spinal segment above the point of shear is dislocated posterior to the segment below. It may involve spinous process fractures.
- Flexion distraction fractures are similar to seatbelt injuries, and result in failure of the posterior and middle columns; but unlike seatbelt injuries, these often result in tearing of the annulus fibrosis, which allows the vertebra above to dislocate.

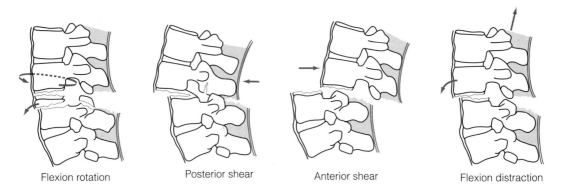

Flexion rotation   Posterior shear   Anterior shear   Flexion distraction

Figure 7.6
Fracture dislocations

Case 52

Patient fell down several steps. Normally painful back, but now increased pain.

Is there an injury?

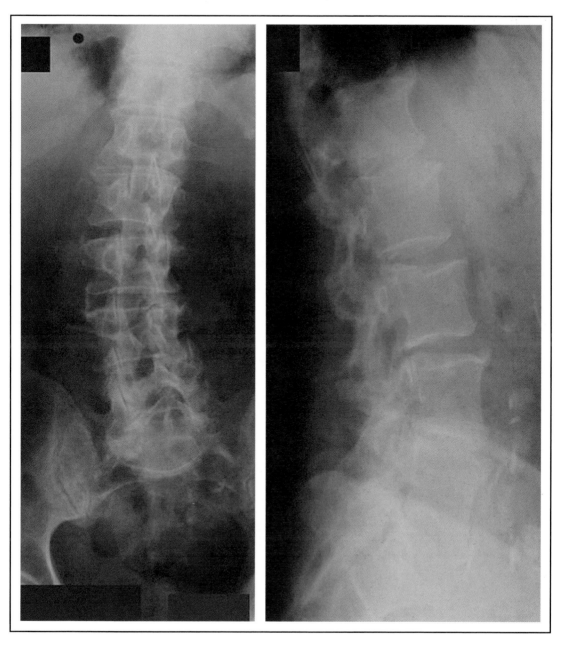

Answer to Case 52

The patient has known degenerative changes of the spine, with a scoliosis concave to the right. Obtaining a true lateral view of the spine was difficult due to the scoliosis and the patient's increased pain; this, along with the altered radiographic appearance of the spine due to degenerative changes, makes interpretation of the radiograph and the search for fractures difficult. On closer observation there is a step in the anterior and superior cortex of lumbar vertebra 3 with a sclerotic line, which are the signs of a fracture.

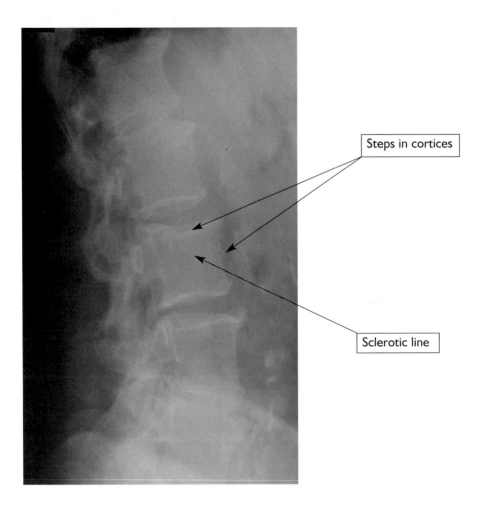

Steps in cortices

Sclerotic line

Case 53

Elderly lady with known osteoporosis. Increased pain in spine following a fall.

Describe the radiographs.

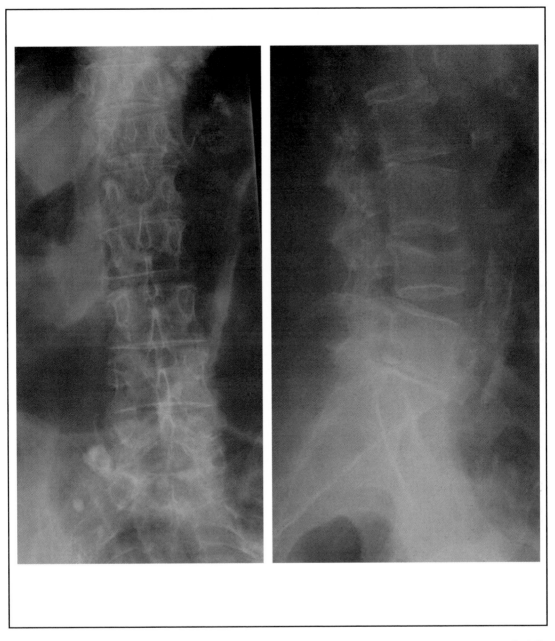

Answer to Case 53

There is a wedge fracture at lumbar vertebra 4, with a buckle at its anterior superior aspect. Sometimes in osteoporotic patients it can be difficult or impossible to assess on plain radiographs whether a wedge fracture is old and chronic or new and acute. The difference between new and old wedge fractures in these types of patients may have to be diagnosed clinically.

Case 54

Young patient fell off motorbike, now has pain in back.

Describe the radiographs.

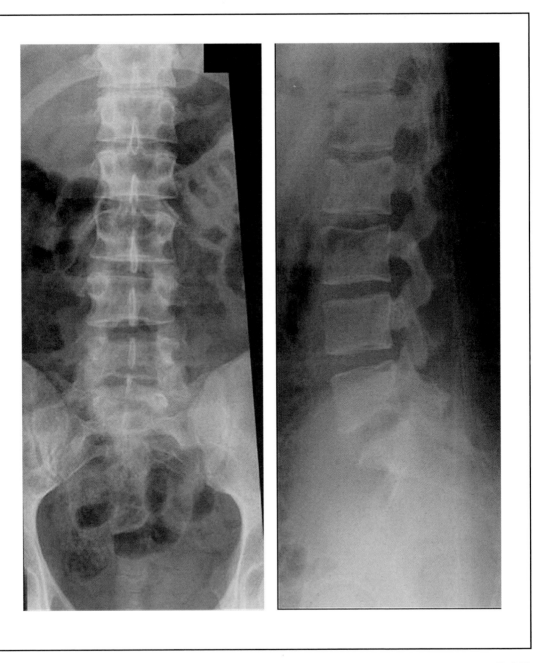

Answer to Case 54

There is a fracture of the superior anterior aspect of lumbar vertebra 2. This is a similar type of injury to that in Case 52, but this time it is easier to view, as a true lateral radiograph of the spine was possible and the patient does not have degenerative changes.

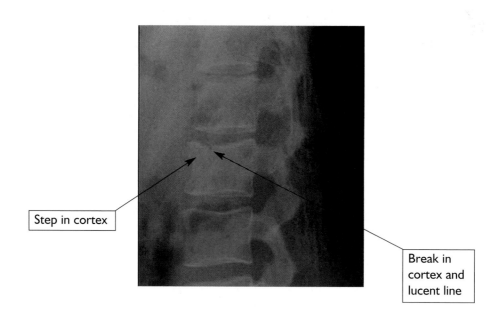

Step in cortex

Break in cortex and lucent line

Case 55

Patient has had severe back pain for several days following minor trauma.

Is there an injury?

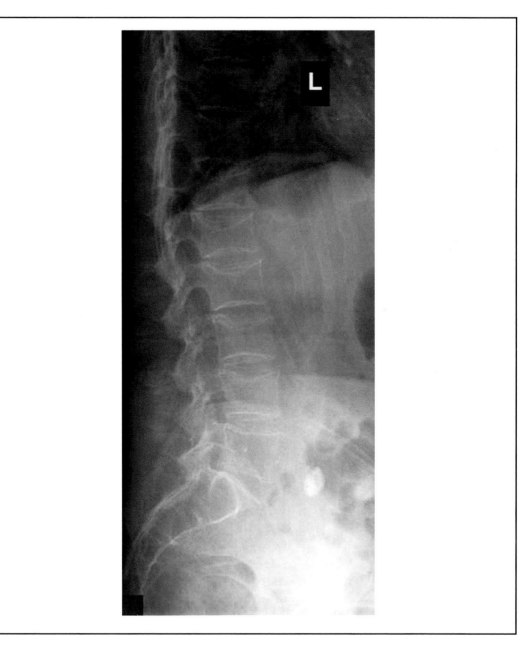

Answer to Case 55

There are superior end plate fractures of lumbar vertebrae 1–4. The patient's bone structure on these radiographs appears osteoporotic. Such severe injuries of several vertebrae following a minor fall leads one to suspect a pathological cause of the fractures. The radiologist's report suggested the clinician should test for myeloma as the pathological cause of these fractures.

Case 56

Patient unable to walk, and has severe pain following a fall.

Describe the radiographs.

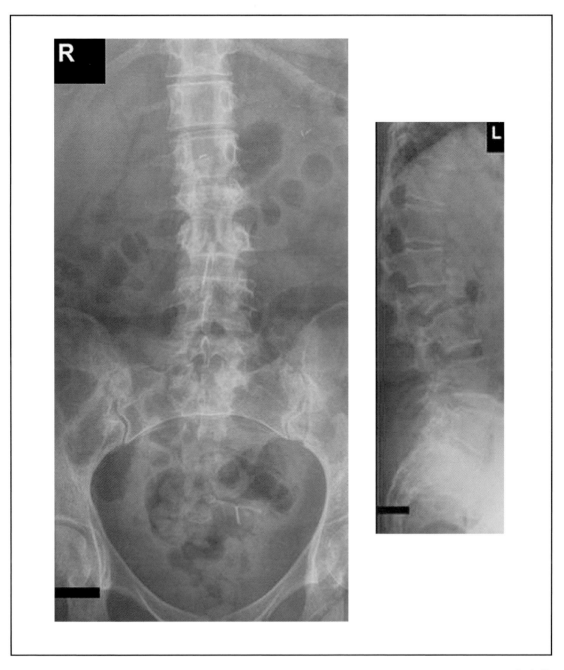

Answer to Case 56

There appears to be a burst fracture of lumbar vertebra 2, with complete destruction and collapse of the vertebra and retropulsion of bone fragments. The patient had a history of renal cell tumour, with secondaries in the vertebra. Hence it is probably a combination of the trauma and pathology that has led to complete destruction and collapse of the vertebra.

Case 57

Patient fell down several steps, now has pain in lower back.

Is there an injury?

Comment on the appearance of the coccyx.

Is it normal practice to x-ray for injury to the coccyx?

What is the normal mechanism of injury for a fractured coccyx?

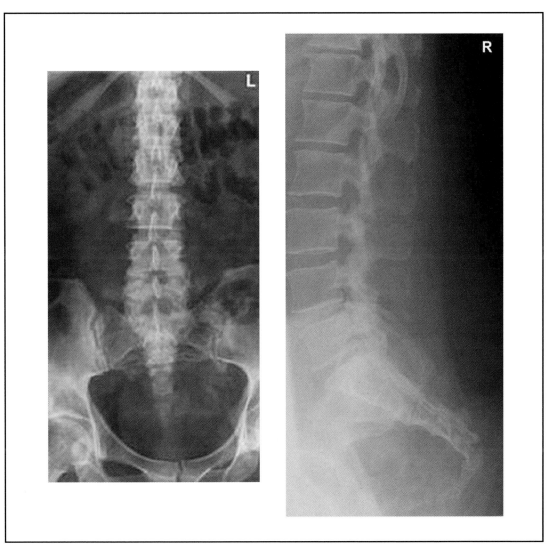

Answer to Case 57

There is no trauma demonstrated on these radiographs. There is severe anteversion of the coccyx. It is not normal protocol to x-ray for injury to the coccyx; it is not recommended by the Royal College of Radiologists (2003), *Making the Best Use of a Department of Clinical Radiology*. Normally fracture of the coccyx is a clinical diagnosis; anterior angulation of the coccyx is frequent in normal adults and not a sign of fracture. The most common mechanisms of injury for a fractured coccyx are falling in a sitting position and vaginal delivery.

Case 58

Patient has chronic backache, which is getting worse.

Describe the radiograph.

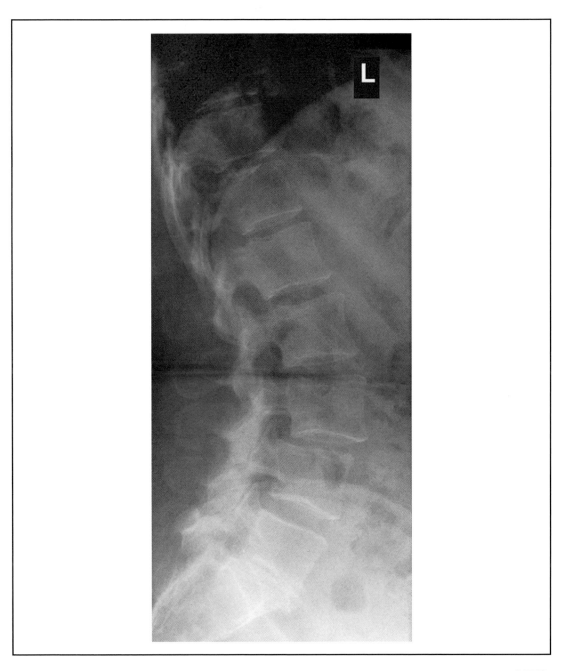

Answer to Case 58

There is spondylolisthesis, grade 1 at lumbar vertebrae 4/5.

There appears to be step-off of the spinous processes above the slip, which is more likely to be due to a true spondylolisthesis (see pages 149–152). There does appear to be a faint lucent line of the pars interarticularis at this level.

Case 59

Longstanding pain in back, now appears worse. Patient has known osteoporosis.

Describe the radiographs.

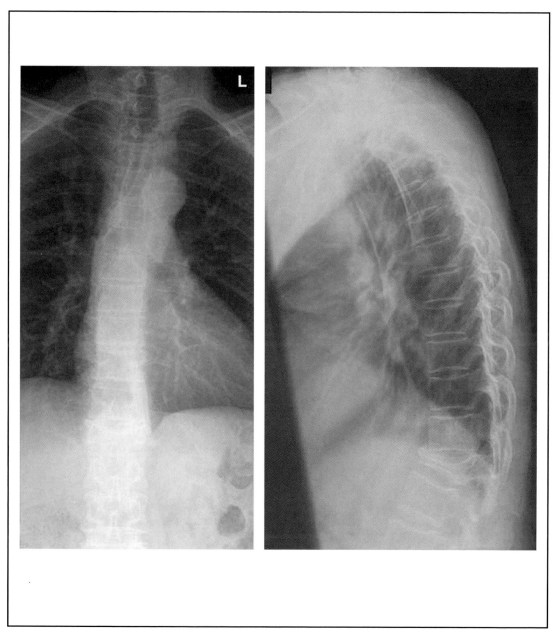

Answer to Case 59

There is anterior vertebral collapse, of dorsal vertebra 12, which is probably osteoporotic collapse.

Case 60

Another patient with longstanding back pain, which is getting worse.

Is there an abnormality?

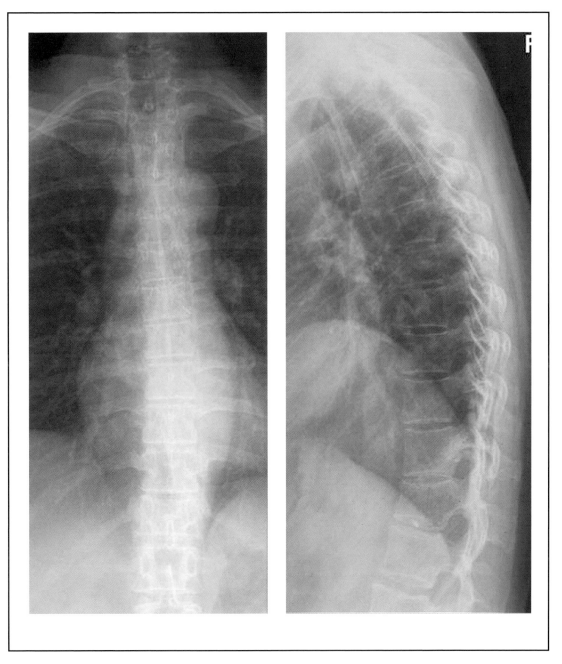

Answer to Case 60

There is loss of vertebral height of dorsal vertebra 12.

8.

Skull, mandibular and facial trauma

Case 61

Patient fell down steps, and banged head. Patient thinks he lost consciousness. Difficult to obtain accurate history of incident, severe soft tissue swelling and bruising at site of trauma.

Describe the radiographs.

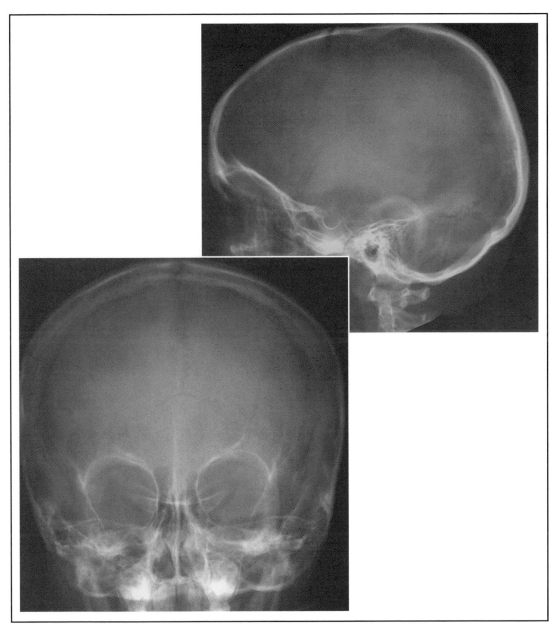

Answer to Case 61

There is a fracture of the right parietal bone.

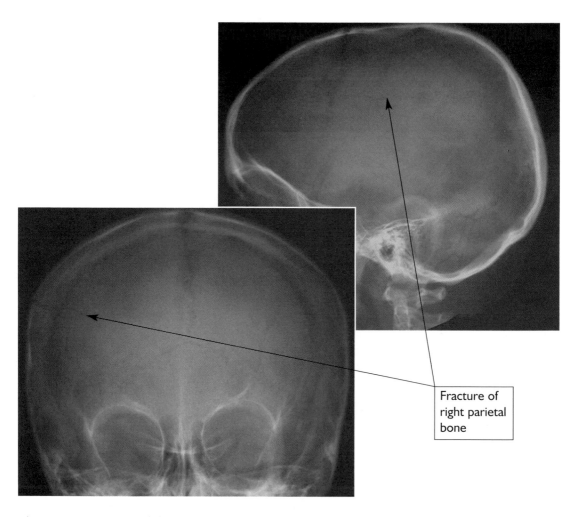

Fracture of right parietal bone

The NICE (2003) guidelines for assessment and management of head injuries advocate that skull radiographs are only needed where CT is not available or in children when there is a suspicion of non-accidental injury. Hence we are seeing fewer skull radiographs these days, so I have only included a few skull cases.

Vascular markings on skull radiographs may be mistaken for fractures. In general fractures of the skull appear densely black (this is due to both the inner and outer tables being involved), do not taper or have branches that taper, and do not have sclerotic margins. Vascular markings tend to appear grey on radiographs (as vessels lie in grooves in the inner table of the skull), have branches that decrease in size and have sclerotic margins.

Case 62

Describe the radiographs.

Comment on the position of the normal sutures.

Name some of the additional sutures that may be found.

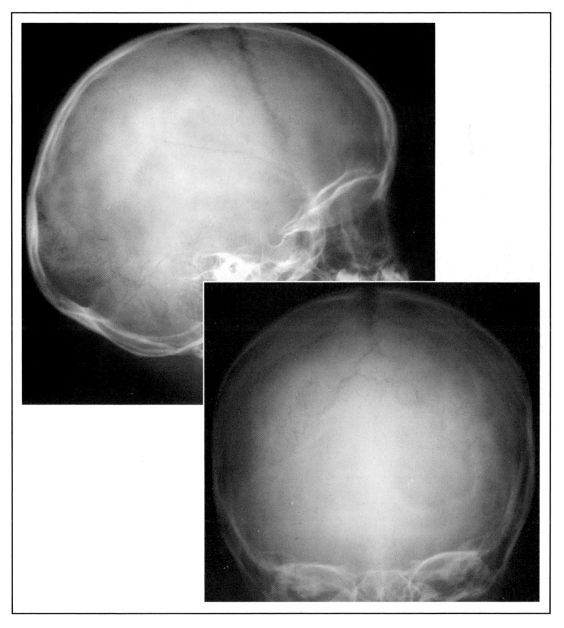

Answer to Case 62

There is a simple linear fracture of the parietal bone, demonstrated on the lateral radiograph. The additional importance of this is that the middle meningeal artery lies in this region and may be injured, leading to an intercranial bleed.

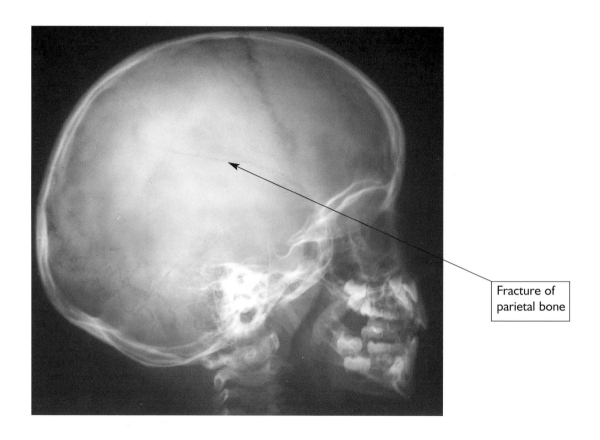

Fracture of parietal bone

The normal sutures found on skull radiographs are the sagittal, coronal, lamboidal, squamosal, occipitomastoid. Common accessory sutures are the metopic suture (commonest accessory suture may persist into adult, divides frontal bone into two halves), accessory parietal suture may be incomplete, may be vertical, horizontal or oblique), mendosal suture (extends posteriorly from lamboidal suture on lateral view, passes medially on Towne's view) and innominate suture (this is always present in infants, and disappears as child matures).

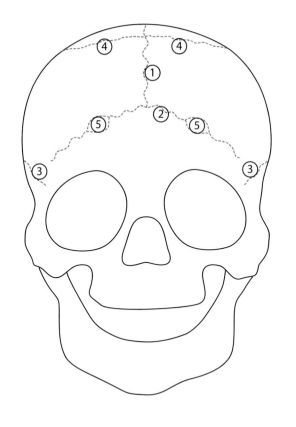

Figure 8.1
Normal sutures on anterior posterior radiograph

1 Sagittal suture

2 Lamboidal suture

3 Squamosal suture

4 Coronal suture

5 Wormian bone

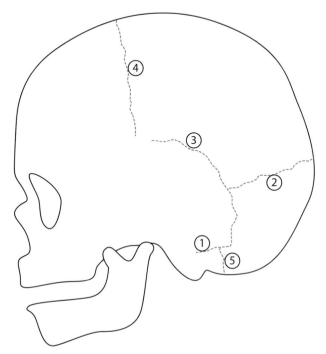

Figure 8.2
Normal sutures on lateral radiograph

1 Occipitomastoid suture

2 Lamboidal suture

3 Squamousal suture

4 Coronal suture

5 Innominate suture

185

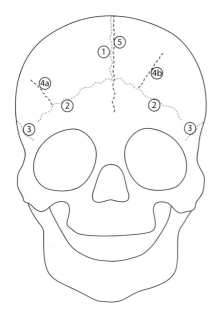

Figure 8.3

Possible positions of accessory sutures on anterior posterior radiograph

1 Sagittal suture

2 Lamboidal suture

3 Squamosal suture

4a Accessory parietal suture

4b Accessory parietal suture

5 Metopic suture

Figure 8.4

Possible positions of parietal accessory sutures on lateral radiograph

1 Occipitomastoid suture

2 Lamboidal suture

3 Squamosal suture

4 Coronal suture

5 Innominate suture

A A complete horizontal accessory parietal suture

B, C Incomplete accessory parietal sutures

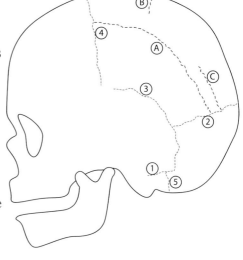

Figure 8.5 **Accessory sutures on a Towne's radiograph**

1 Sagittal suture

2 Lamboidal suture

3 Squamosal suture

4 Coronal suture

5 Foramen magnum

6 Mendosal suture (occasionally it is complete as demonstrated here, but more often it is incomplete)

Case 63

Describe the radiographs. Is there an injury?

Why should lateral skull radiographs be taken with a horizontal beam?

The last two cases have demonstrated linear fractures of the skull.

Name another type of fracture of the skull.

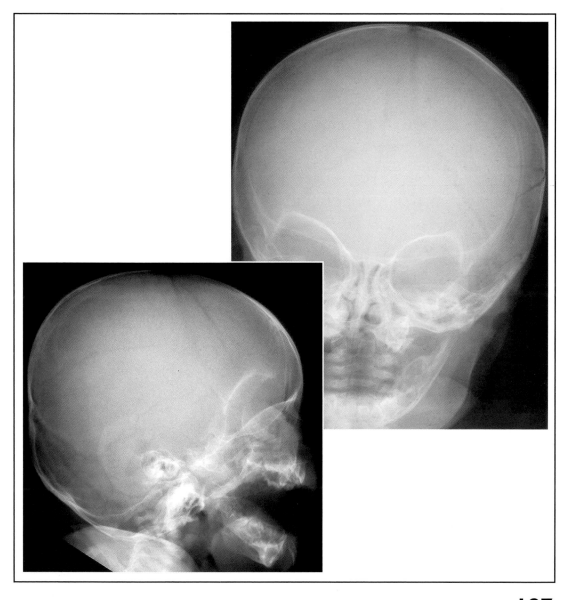

Answer to Case 63

There is a left parietal fracture. Trauma lateral skull radiographs should always be taken with a horizontal beam to ascertain whether there is a fluid level in the sphenoid sinus. This sign would be indicative of a base of skull fracture, and may be the only sign seen radiographically (another reason why CT is preferable). A fracture that communicates with the sphenoid sinus is an open fracture and as such is a cause for concern regarding infections. The other type of fracture of the skull is a depressed fracture, normally caused by a direct impact. The fracture normally appears as a dense or sclerotic area, due to overlying fragments of bone.

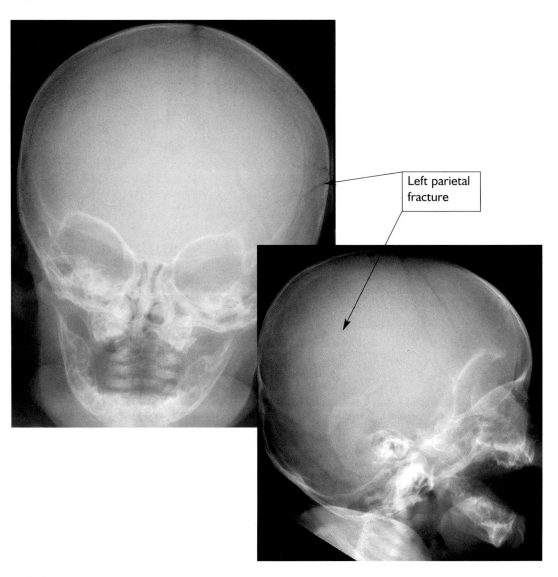

Left parietal fracture

Case 64

Patient was involved in a fight, now unable to open mouth.

Is there an injury?

List the different areas of fractures of the mandible.

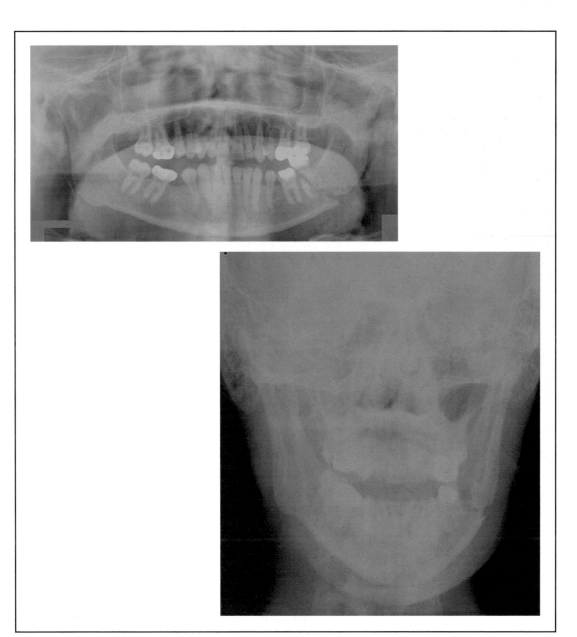

Answer to Case 64

There is a fracture at the left angle of the mandible involving a molar tooth (actually fracturing through the tooth).

The mandible can be subdivided into several regions:
● the ramus, which lies between the angle of the mandible and the base of the coronoid and condylar processes
● the body, which extends between the canine tooth anteriorly and the angle of the mandible posteriorly
● the symphysis, which lies between the two canine teeth.

The different areas of fracture of the mandible are as listed below:
● Condyles – are they extracapsular or intracapsular?
● Angle
● Body
● Parasymphysis
● Symphysis
● Alveolar
● Coronoid
● Ramus.

The mandible is like a bony ring so, as with other areas of the body that are bony rings, if you see one fracture look for another. The most common radiographs for trauma mandibles are a posterior anterior view and an OPG (orthopantogram); where an OPG machine is not available the normal practice is for a posterior anterior view and two oblique mandible views to be taken.

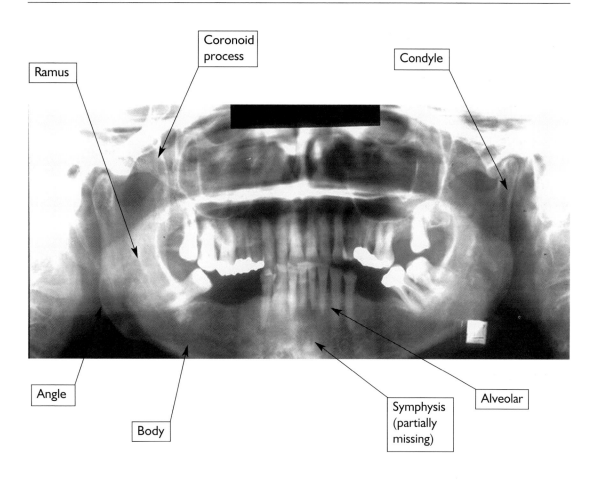

Coronoid process

Condyle

Ramus

Angle

Body

Symphysis (partially missing)

Alveolar

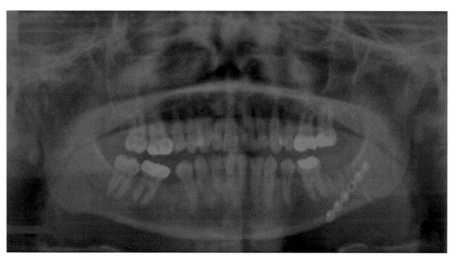

Post-operative panoramic view of patient from this case

Some of the clinical signs the referring clinician will be looking for prior to sending the patient for an x-ray of their mandible are listed below.

Clinical features of a fractured mandible:
- Local swelling, bruising and tenderness
- Intraoral haemorrhage
- Drooling
- Step in the occlusion or at the lower border
- Bleeding from the ear
- Mobility of the fragments
- Sublingual ecchymosis
- Trismus
- Mobile teeth
- Mental anaesthesia/parathesia.

Case 65

Describe the radiograph.

What are favourable and unfavourable fractures of the mandible?

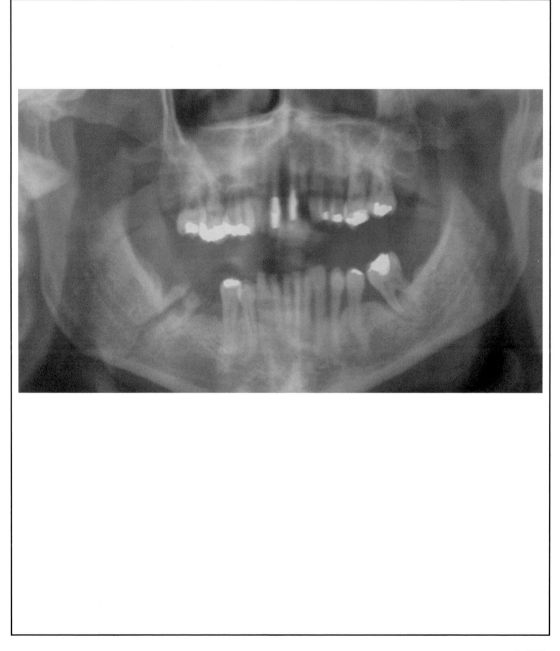

Answer to Case 65

There is a fracture of the right body of the mandible, again involving the tooth.

Mandibular fractures are favourable or unfavourable depending whether they are distracted or not, due to the muscle pull and the direction of the fracture line. In favourable fractures, the associated muscles tend to hold the fragments together; in unfavourable fractures, the associated muscles tend to pull the fractures apart. This determines management of the patient. The muscles involved are the masseter and the medial pterygoid. The horizontal pull of the masseter is assessed from the panoramic view, the vertical pull of the medial pterygoid is assessed from the PA (posterior anterior view of the mandible (see Figure 8.7).

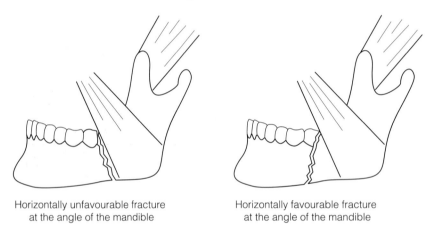

Horizontally unfavourable fracture   Horizontally favourable fracture
at the angle of the mandible   at the angle of the mandible

Figure 8.7 **Favourable and unfavourable fractures**

Some of the issues the maxillary facial team will be looking for on the mandible radiographs in order to plan treatment are listed below.

Assessment of the mandible radiographs

- Degree of fracture displacement; does it need active treatment?
- If the fracture is undisplaced, is it likely to become unstable? Is the muscle pull favourable or unfavourable?
- Does the fracture involve the teeth? If the fracture involves the teeth then it is an open fracture with a risk of infection.
- Should the teeth be extracted or not?
- Is there space for plates?
- Is early mobilisation required?

Case 66

Patient has longstanding pain in mandible, which has increased following a fall.

Describe the radiograph.

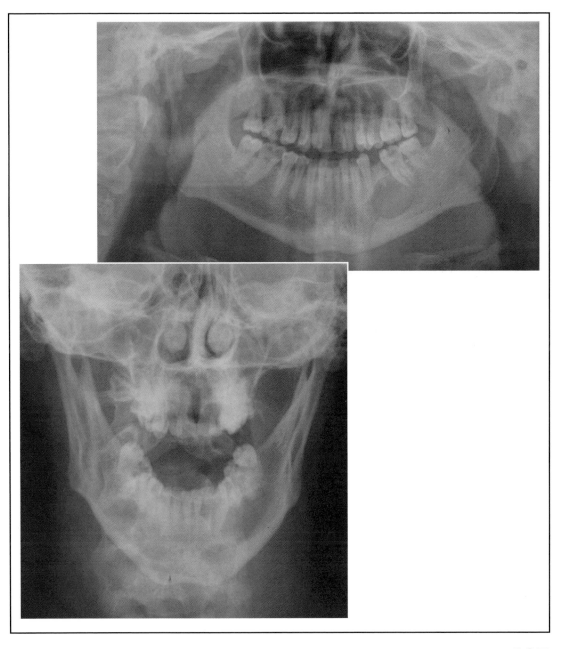

Answer to Case 66

There is an abcess in the left parasymphysis area with a fracture transversing its inferior edge.

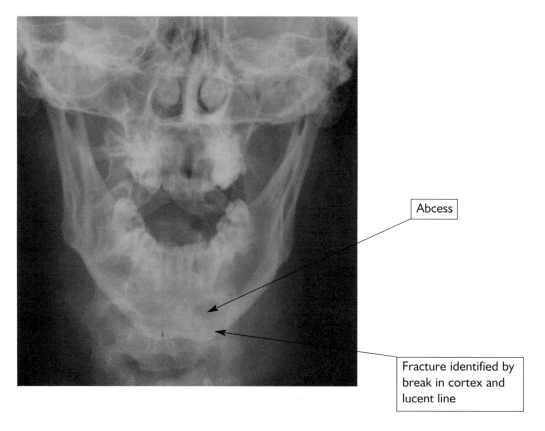

Abcess

Fracture identified by break in cortex and lucent line

When reviewing mandible radiographs for fracture, it is useful to have a check list of signs of fracture to look for.

Radiological signs of fracture

- Step in cortex. Look carefully at lower border of mandible.
- Step in occlusal plane.
- Usually a radiolucent line, which may appear double due to buccal and lingual cortices.
- If the fracture has overlapping fragments then a radio-opaque line will be seen.
- Beware of air shadows mimicking fractures, particularly at the angle of the mandible
- If there is a fracture at one side always check for a fracture at the other side.

Case 67

Patient fell on to mandible.

Is there an injury?

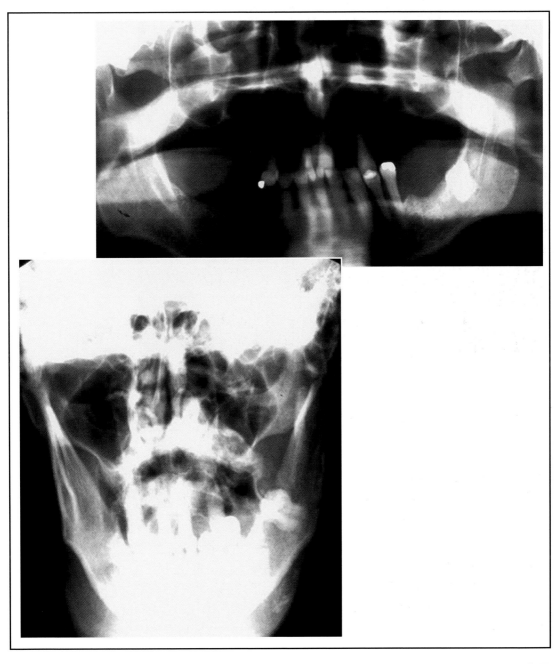

Answer to Case 67

There is a fracture of the left condyle, demonstrated on both radiographs.

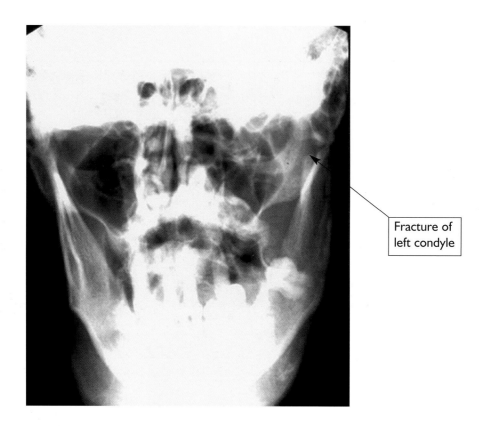

Fracture of
left condyle

Case 68

Soldier fainted while on guard duty, falling forward on to mandible.

Describe the radiographs.

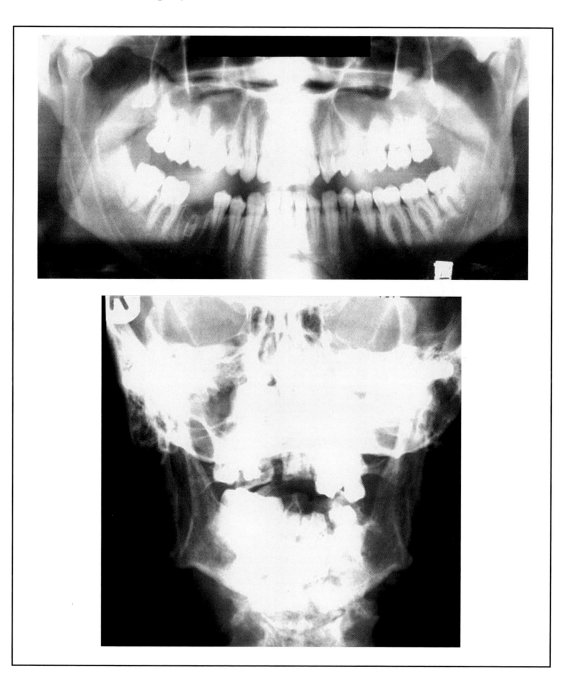

Answer to Case 68

There is a fracture of the left parasymphysis, demonstrated on both radiographs. These fractures can be very difficult to visualise radiographically, often being only clearly visualised on one radiograph.

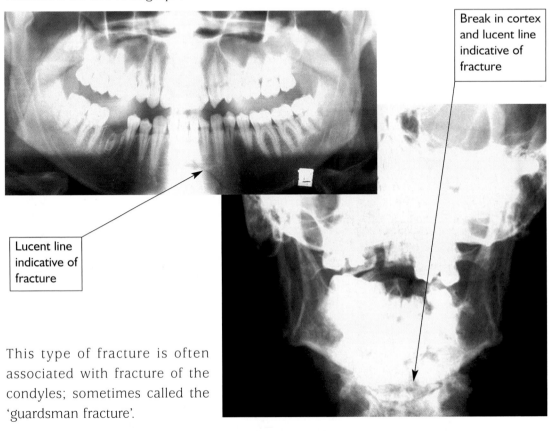

Break in cortex and lucent line indicative of fracture

Lucent line indicative of fracture

This type of fracture is often associated with fracture of the condyles; sometimes called the 'guardsman fracture'.

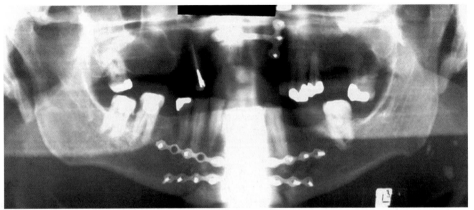

Patient postoperative

200

Case 69

Patient fell directly on to mandible, now unable to open and close mouth.

Describe the radiographs.

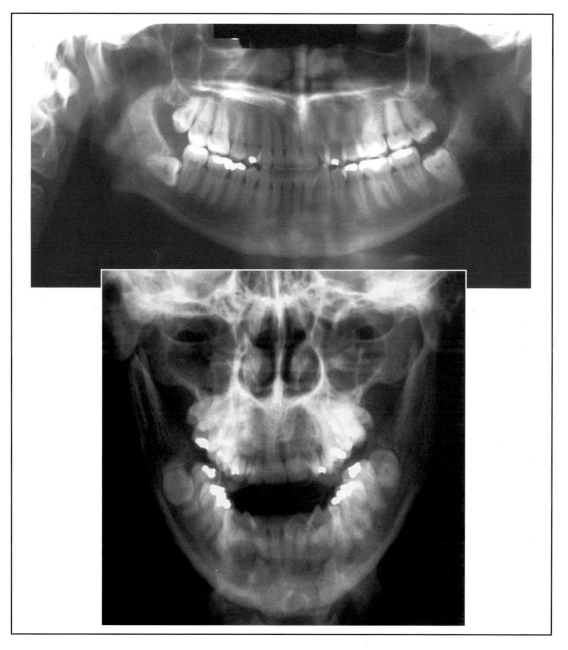

Answer to Case 69

There are fractures of the right and left condyles and the left symphysis. These injuries are more clearly demonstrated on the PA mandible, demonstrating the importance of always doing more than one view. These injuries are typical of the 'guardsman' injury.

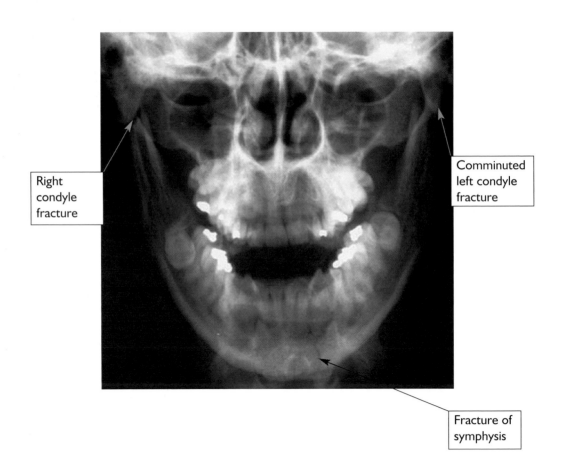

Right condyle fracture

Comminuted left condyle fracture

Fracture of symphysis

Case 70

Patient was involved in a road traffic accident, injuring the face.

Describe the radiographs.

Comment on the lines that are utilised when reviewing facial trauma.

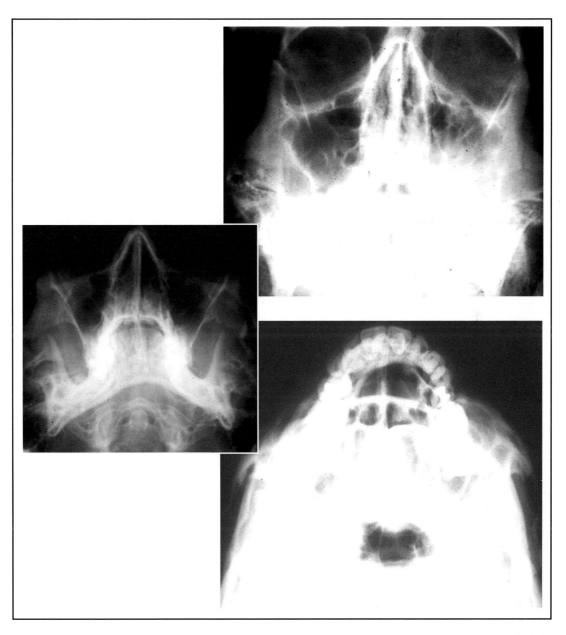

Answer to Case 70

There is a fracture of the left zygomatic arch, a step in the inferior border of the left orbit (indicative of fracture of the body of the zygoma), and probable widening of the left frontozygomatic suture. This combination of injuries is the classic tripod fracture. A tripod fracture consists of widening of the frontozygomatic suture, fracture of the zygomatic arch and fracture through the body of the zygoma (sometimes demonstrated on the radiograph as a fracture of the inferior border of the orbit and/or a fracture of the lateral aspect of the maxillary sinus). The tripod fracture is now called a zygomaticomaxillary complex fracture, and is so called because it involves separation of all three major attachments of the zygoma to the rest of the face. This is a very old case, which includes a submentovertical (SMV) view of the facial bones to demonstrate the fracture of the zygomatic arch. This view is no longer routinely done.

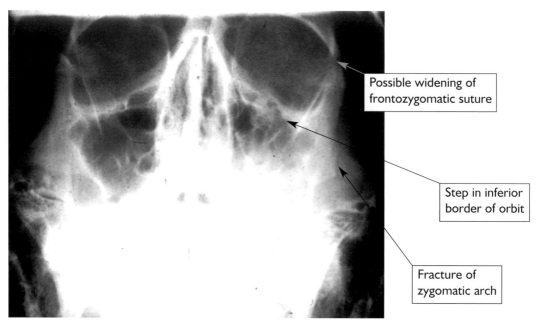

Possible widening of frontozygomatic suture

Step in inferior border of orbit

Fracture of zygomatic arch

Occipitomental view (OM)

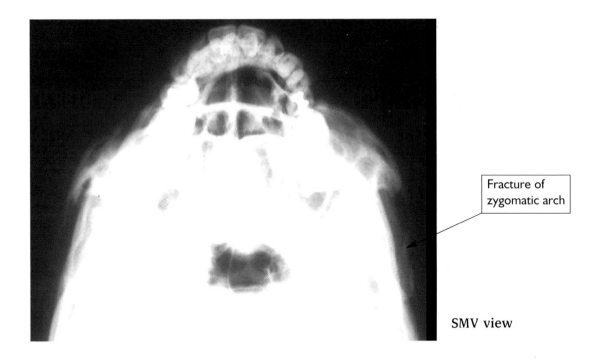

Fracture of
zygomatic arch

SMV view

Fractures of the facial bones can be classified as to whether they involve the central middle third, involving nasal/nasoethmoidal maxillary area or the lateral middle third, malar type fractures; the latter can be classified as shown below.

Classification of malar fractures
- **Type I**   undisplaced
- **Type II**   zygomatic arch fractures
- **Type III**   tripod fracture with frontozygomatic suture intact
- **Type IV**   tripod fracture with frontozygomatic suture distracted
- **Type V**   orbital floor blowout with or without type III,IV, VII
- **TypeVI**   orbital rim fracture
- **Type VII** comminuted and complex fracture.

Hence this fracture is either a Type III or IV malar fracture depending whether the fronto-zygomatic suture is intact or not.

When reviewing facial trauma radiographs it is helpful to have a system of review to prevent fractures being missed. McGrigor and Dolan's lines are shown overleaf (Figures 8.8 and 8.9). Line 4 is mainly to draw attention to the mandible.

Line 1 – *links the right and left supra-orbital margins across the frontal sinus.* Look along this line for widening of the frontozygomatic sutures, and for fluid levels in the frontal sinuses.

Line 2 – *joins both frontozygomatic processes passing through the base of the ethmoid sinuses and the infra-orbital margins.* Look along this line for fractures of the zygomatic arch, inferior rim of orbits.

Line 3 – *joins both tempero-zygomatic processes through the base of the maxilla and nasal septa.* Look along this line for a fracture of the zygoma and lateral aspect of the maxillary antrum.

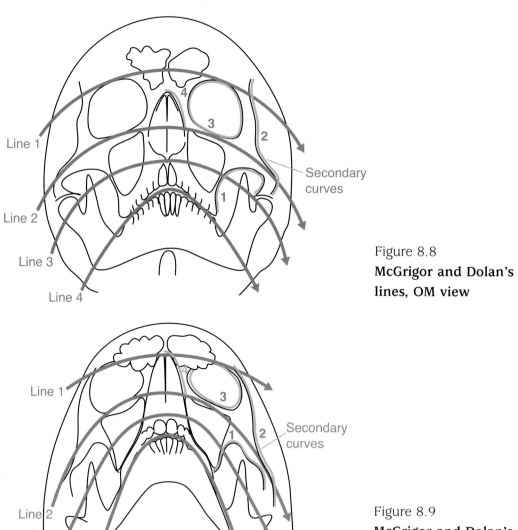

Figure 8.8
McGrigor and Dolan's lines, OM view

Figure 8.9
McGrigor and Dolan's lines, OM 30-degree view

Case 71

Patient was involved in a road traffic accident.

Describe the injuries.

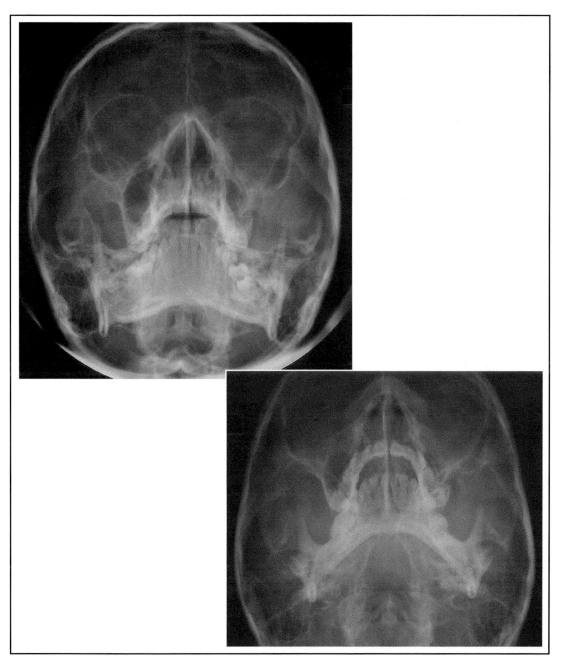

Answer to Case 71

There is a fracture of the lateral wall of the maxillary antra. When reviewing facial bones remember there are two sides to compare; it can be helpful to compare the maxillary sinuses – a fluid filled one can be indicative of a fracture as it fills with blood, but remember it could also be a sign of sinusitis. There is also a fracture of the left zygomatic arch; this is the zygomaticomaxillary complex fracture (see pages 203–206).

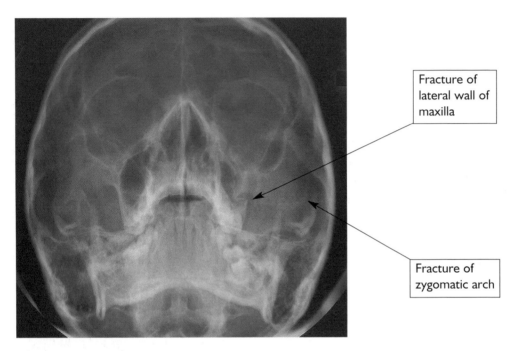

Fracture of lateral wall of maxilla

Fracture of zygomatic arch

Some texts suggest checking the 'elephant's head' for fracture. These in fact are the secondary curves demonstrated in Case 70.

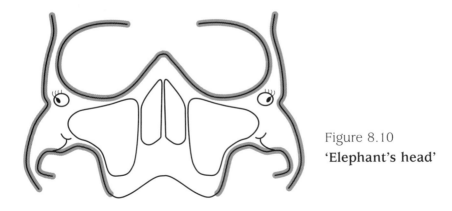

Figure 8.10
'Elephant's head'

Case 72

Cricket ball went into patient's eye, now difficulty seeing, swelling and subconjunctive haemorrhage.

Describe the radiograph.

Comment on another non-bony sign of this injury.

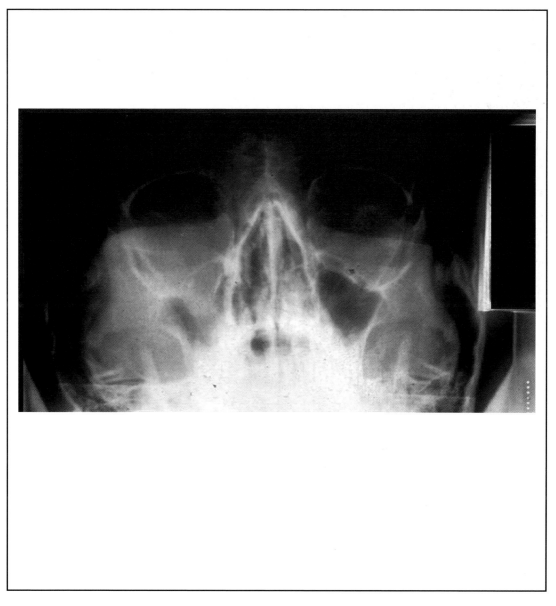

Answer to Case 72

This a blow-out fracture of the right orbit. These injuries normally follow direct impact to the eye (in this case from a ball), causing a fracture of the weakest point of the orbital walls due to pressure from the surrounding fat pads and rectus muscle. If the clinician requests radiographs for this injury, then the most common views taken are the standard OM view and angled OM view (often angled caudally by 30 degrees) in order to demonstrate the inferior orbital area. As the orbital contents herniate downwards through the fractured orbital floor they create a radio-opaque teardrop as demonstrated in this case. Another sign of this injury is the 'black eyebrow sign'. An ethmoid or maxillary fracture allows air to escape from the sinus which will rise to the superior aspect of the orbit – resulting in 'the black eyebrow' sign. This is an old case, and below is a tomogram of the orbits, clearly demonstrating the radiographic teardrop. Today a CT scan would be carried out.

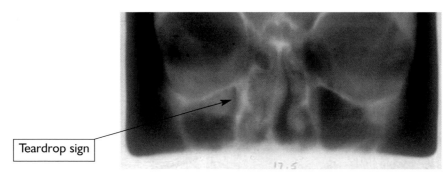

Teardrop sign

Figure 8.11 **Tomogram of the orbits**

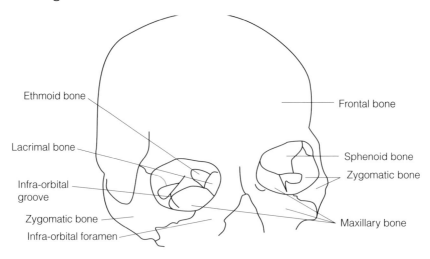

Ethmoid bone

Frontal bone

Lacrimal bone

Sphenoid bone

Zygomatic bone

Infra-orbital groove

Zygomatic bone

Maxillary bone

Infra-orbital foramen

Figure 8.12 **Anatomy of the orbit demonstrating the thin portion of the floor of the orbit, posterior to the thick orbital rim**

210

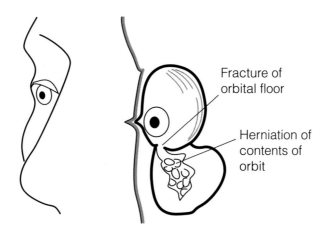

Fracture of
orbital floor

Herniation of
contents of
orbit

Figure 8.13
Blow-out fracture of the orbit, demonstrating herniation of contents of orbit to form radio-opaque teardrop

Case 73

Patient had direct hit to eye.

Is there any sign of injury?

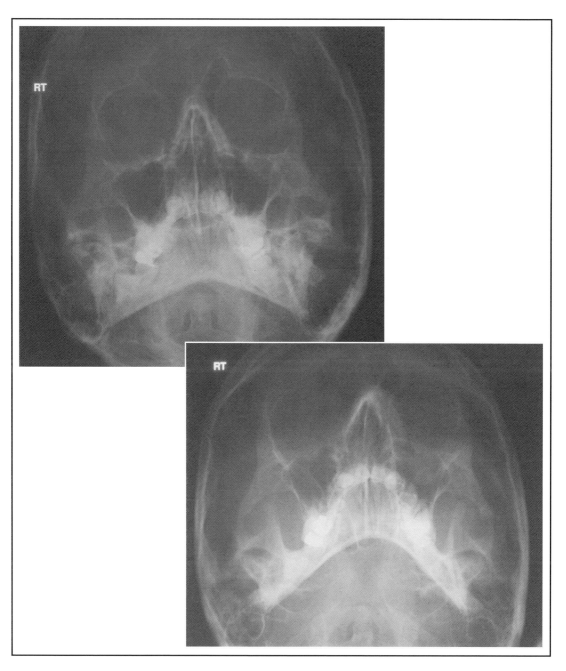

Answer to Case 73

A radio-opaque teardrop is demonstrated below the left orbit, indicative of a blow-out fracture of the left orbit, (see pages 209–211.

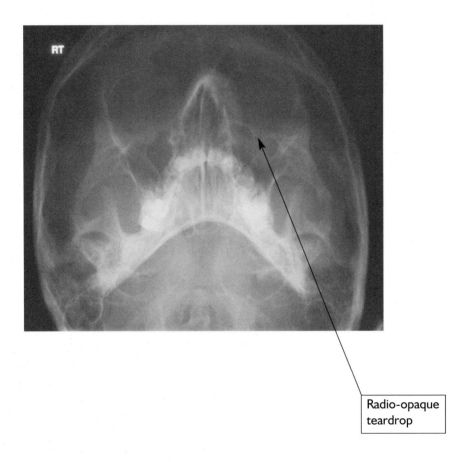

Radio-opaque teardrop

Case 74

Patient was involved in a road traffic accident.

Describe the injuries.

Comment on Lefort type fractures.

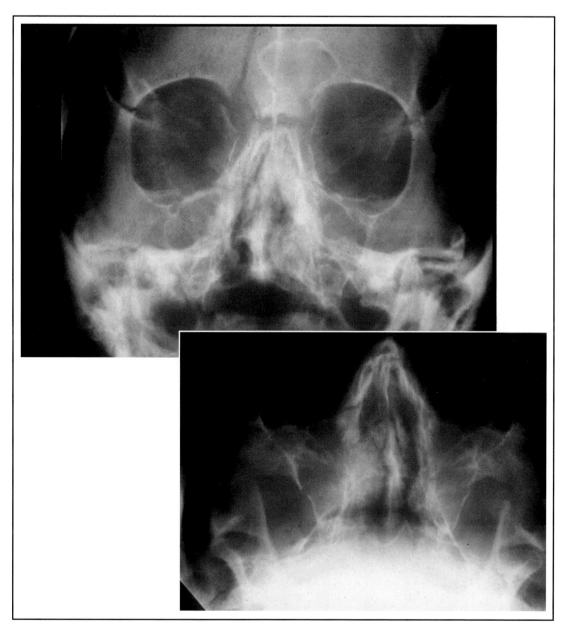

Answer to Case 74

There are several fractures. There is a fracture of the superior orbital rim extending into the frontal bone and probably the frontal sinus. There is widening of the right fronto-zygomatic suture, a fracture across the nasion and fractures of the lateral walls of the maxillary antrum.

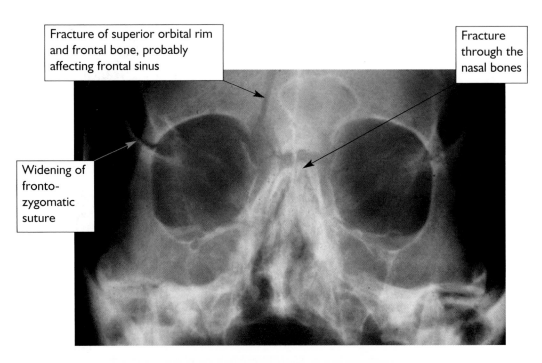

Fracture of superior orbital rim and frontal bone, probably affecting frontal sinus

Fracture through the nasal bones

Widening of fronto-zygomatic suture

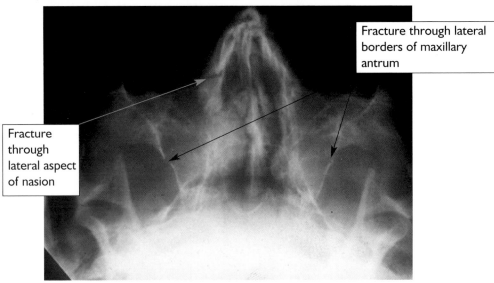

Fracture through lateral borders of maxillary antrum

Fracture through lateral aspect of nasion

The Lefort fracture classification describes fractures of the maxilla, There are three types:

- Lefort I – alveolar separation, a transverse fracture separating the alveolar process from the maxilla. It is sub–zygomatic
- Lefort II – maxillary separation, a pyramidal fracture separating the central portion of the face. Hence sub-zygomatic and pyramidal.
- Lefort III – craniofacial separation; complete separation of the facial skeleton from the skull. It is supra-zygomatic.
- Can be unilateral fractures and combinations of the above with median split.

Hence this patient probably has a Lefort II type injury.

Case 75

Patient was involved in a fight.

Describe the injuries.

Classify using the Lefort classification.

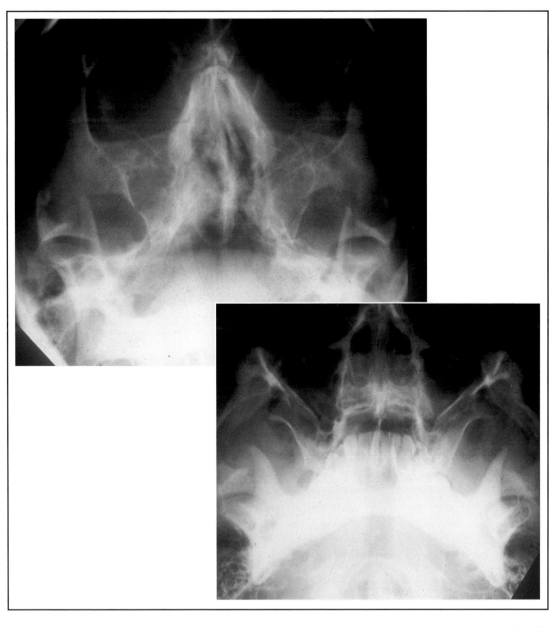

Answer to Case 75

There are fractures of both lateral walls of the maxillary antrum, probable fracture of nasion and a fracture of the left zygoma. This most closely corresponds to a Lefort type II injury.

Probable fracture transversing nasion

Fracture of zygoma

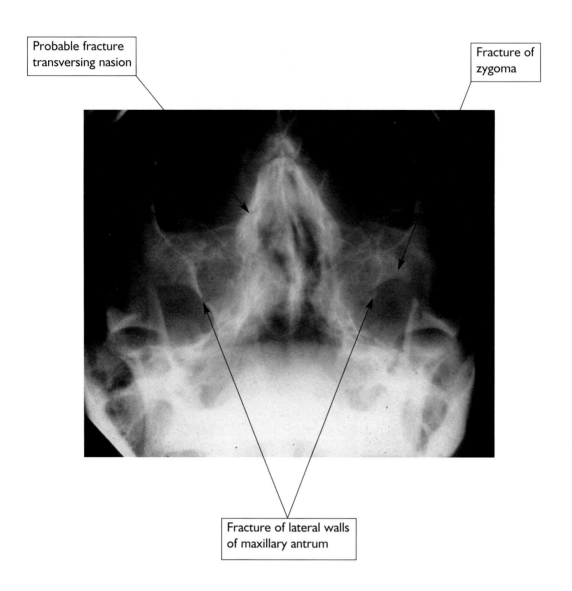

Fracture of lateral walls of maxillary antrum

9.

A selection of cases

Case 76

Elderly lady fell from chair.

Describe the radiographs.

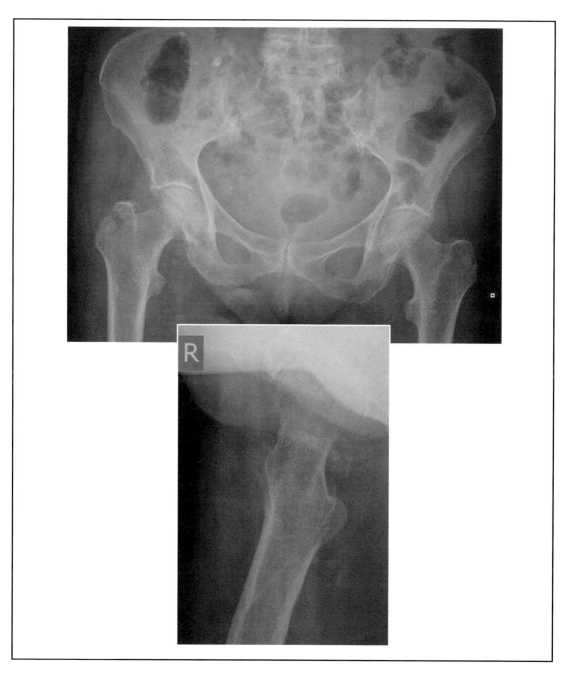

Answer to Case 76

There is a fracture of the right greater trochanter.

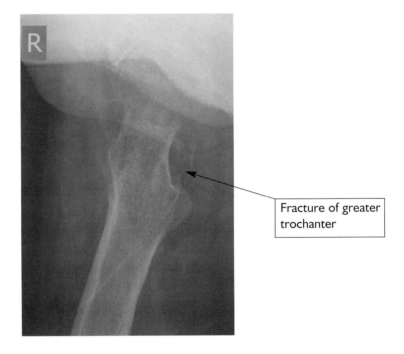

Fracture of greater trochanter

Case 77

Patient was involved in a road traffic accident.

Describe the radiograph.

Are there any injuries?

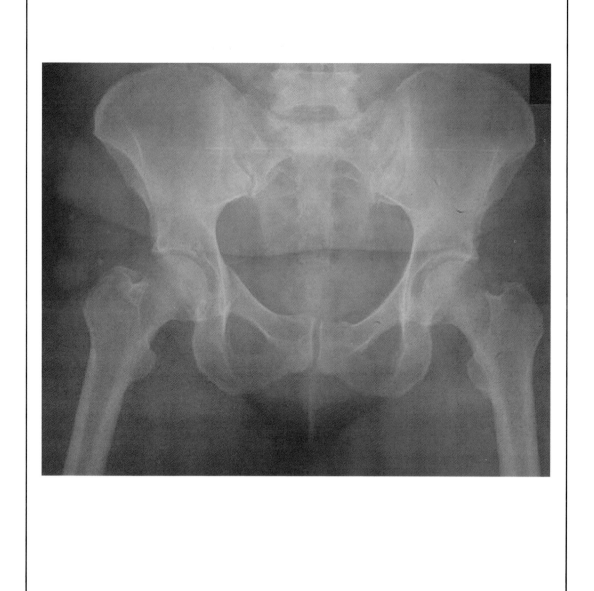

Answer to Case 77

There are several fractures which were confirmed on CT. There are fractures of the right sacral alar, bulging of the right iliopubic line (which is indicative of an acetabular fracture) and a fracture of the left superior pubic ramus.

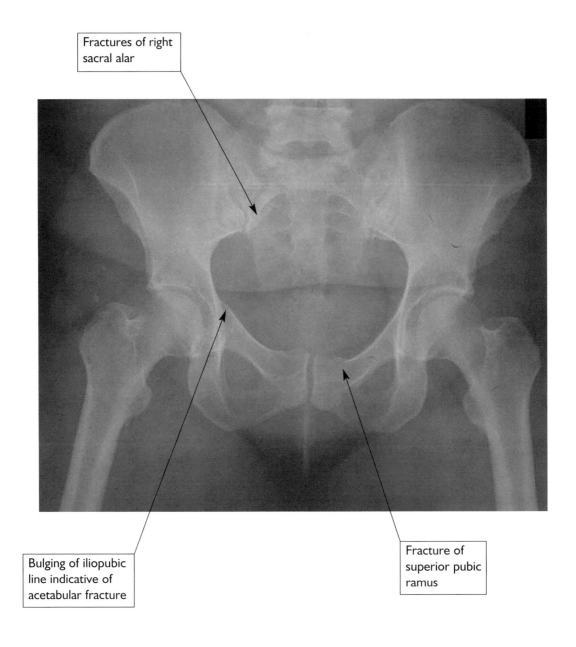

Fractures of right sacral alar

Bulging of iliopubic line indicative of acetabular fracture

Fracture of superior pubic ramus

Case 78

Patient was involved in a road traffic accident.

Lateral cervical spine radiograph was taken in the resuscitation room as part of a trauma series. The antero-posterior and open mouth views were taken later in the x-ray room.

Describe the radiographs.

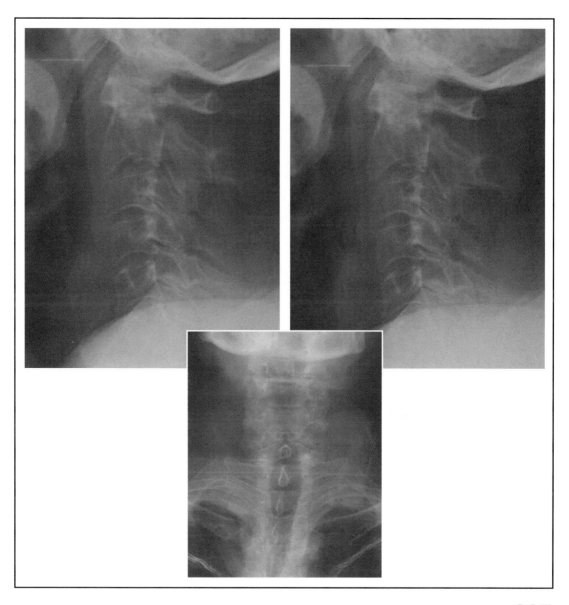

Answer to Case 78

There is an oblique fracture of the body of cervical vertebra 2. It is difficult to ascertain on this lateral view whether the facet joints are involved as it is not a true lateral, but they appear not to be. The lateral view does not demonstrate the lower cervical spine. As mentioned in Chapter 3, if you see one fracture in the cervical spine look for another. This is an extension teardrop. In general an extension teardrop tends to occur at cervical vertebra 2 and the fracture fragment is greater in height than diameter, whereas a flexion teardrop tends to involve the lower cervical spine and the fracture fragment tends to be greater in diameter than height.

Case 79

Patient was involved in a fight.

Describe the injuries.

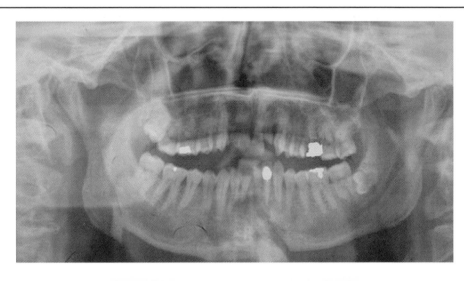

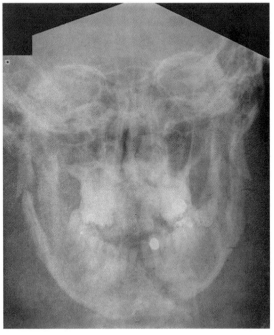

Answer to Case 79

There is an oblique fracture of the right angle of mandible which appears to involve the proximal aspect of the condyle, and is comminuted; there is a comminuted fracture of the left condyle, an oblique fracture of the left parasymphysis moving towards midline and involving the teeth.

Case 80

Patient was experiencing tingling in the hand and neck pain.
On further investigation the patient had injured neck elsewhere
many months ago, had some treatment, then moved away and not
attended any further clinic appointments. Lateral views were
requested to assess any injury, patient was not clear historian.

Describe the radiographs.

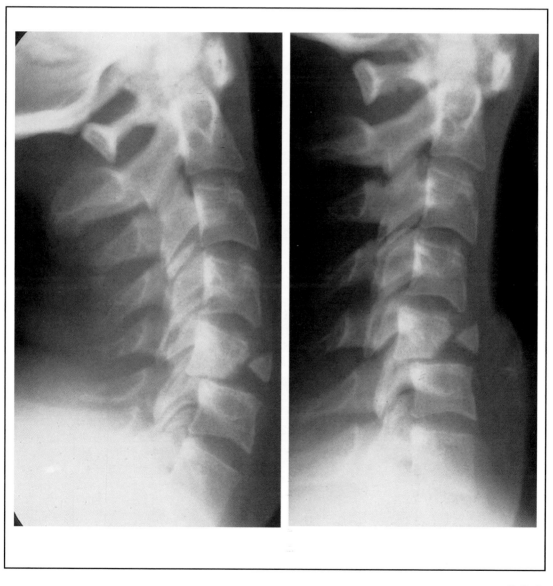

Answer to Case 80

The lateral views demonstrated an old flexion teardrop injury of cervical vertebra 5, with loss of alignment posteriorly. As mentioned previously, if you see one fracture in the cervical spine look for another; for this reason you need to make sure the complete cervical spine is radiographically demonstrated. There is a fracture of the posterior aspect of cervical vertebra 1 with widening of the distance between the odontoid peg and cervical vertebra, indicative of a burst fracture of cervical vertebra 1, the so-called Jefferson's fracture; hence an open mouth view was taken, which confirmed this.

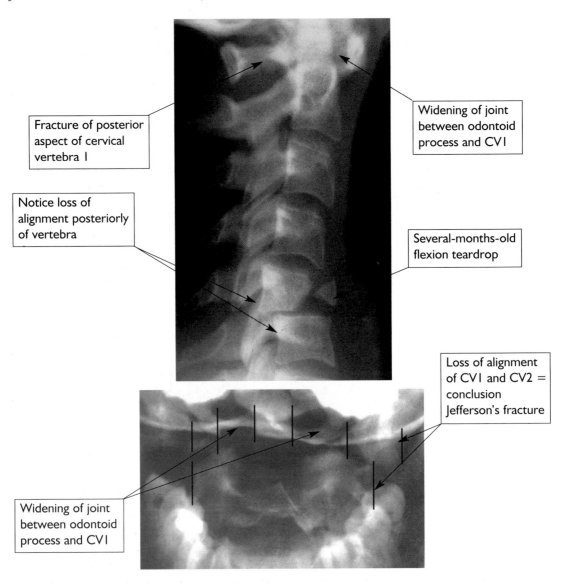

Fracture of posterior aspect of cervical vertebra 1

Widening of joint between odontoid process and CV1

Notice loss of alignment posteriorly of vertebra

Several-months-old flexion teardrop

Loss of alignment of CV1 and CV2 = conclusion Jefferson's fracture

Widening of joint between odontoid process and CV1

Case 81

Patient involved in a road traffic accident.

Describe the radiograph.

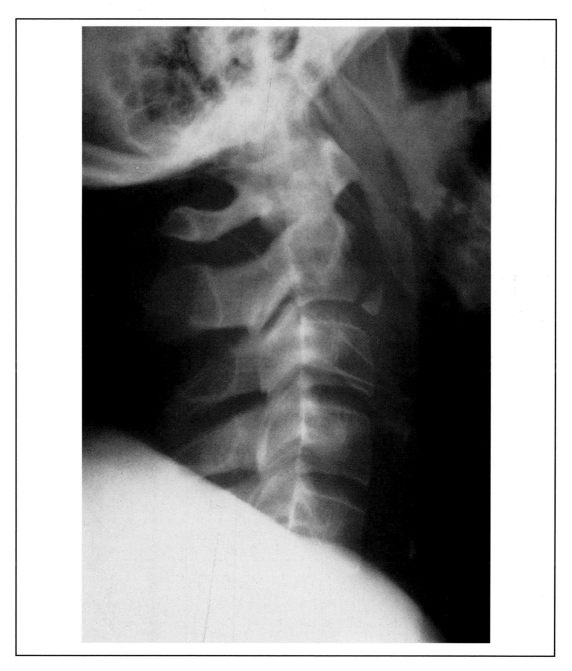

Answer to Case 81

There is a hyperextension teardrop injury of cervical vertebra 2, (see pages 227–228).

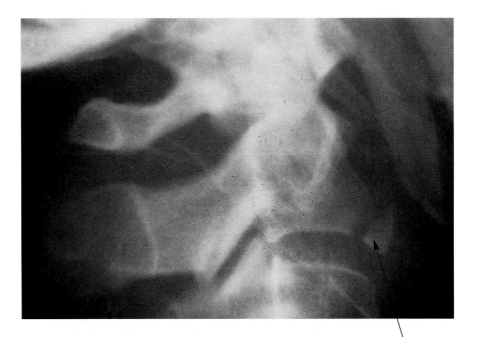

Hyperextension teardrop

Case 82

Elderly lady with long-term problems with neck, fell, injuring neck.

Although the lower cervical spine is not visualised, is there any sign of injury?

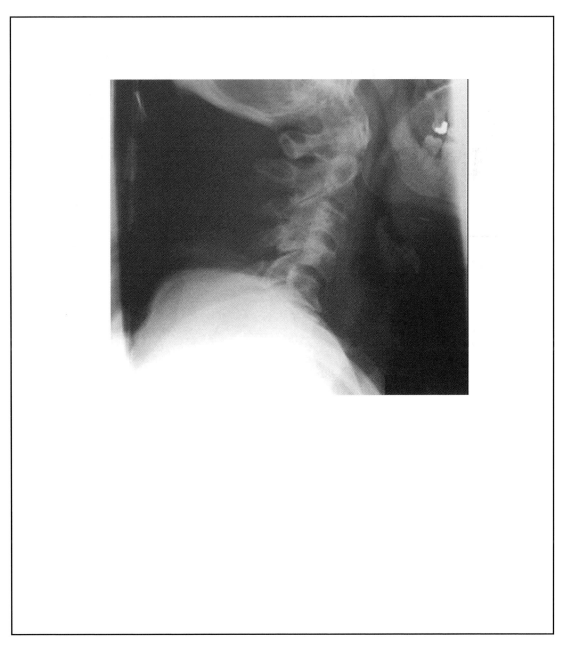

Answer to Case 82

There is loss of alignment at the anterior vertebrae and posteriorly at the facet joints at cervical vertebrae 4/5, indicative of injury. The lateral radiograph below demonstrates how the cervical spine progressed to complete dislocation at cervical vertebrae 4/5 prior to being taken to theatre for stabilisation. This case demonstrates the importance of recognising the subtle signs of cervical spine injury; had these signs not been noticed and the patient had gone home then the complete dislocation may have occurred at home with dire consequences.

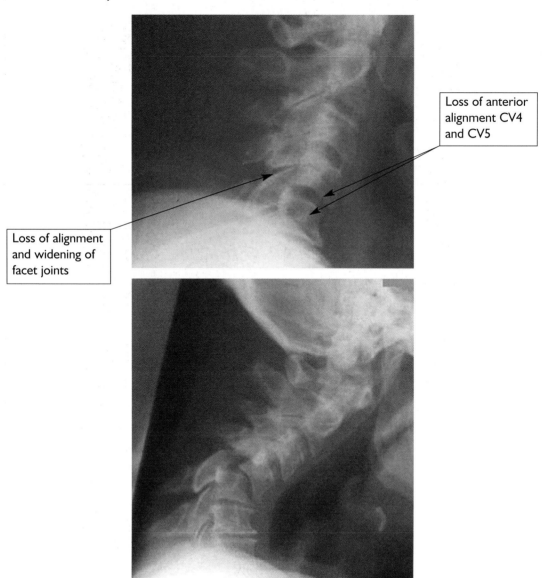

Loss of anterior alignment CV4 and CV5

Loss of alignment and widening of facet joints

Case 83

Patient involved in a road traffic accident.

Describe the radiograph, naming the type of injury, and classifying.

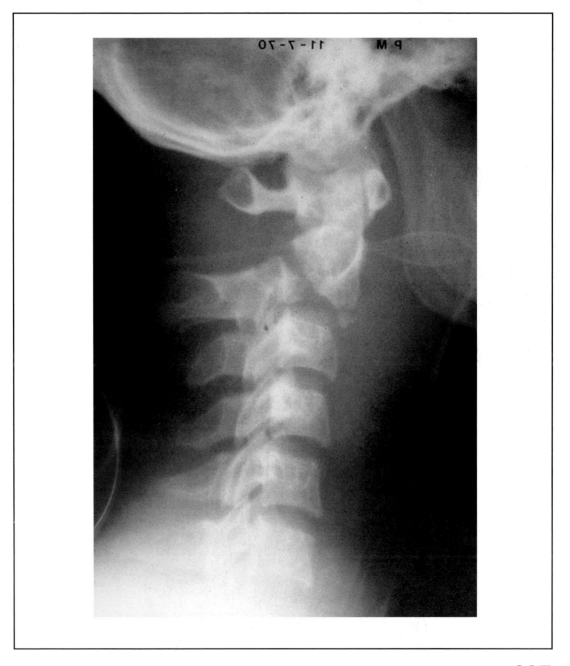

Answer to Case 83

This is a hangman's fracture (fracture of the pars interarticularis) type II with an extension teardrop.

Case 84

Patient fell on to mandible.

Describe the radiographs.

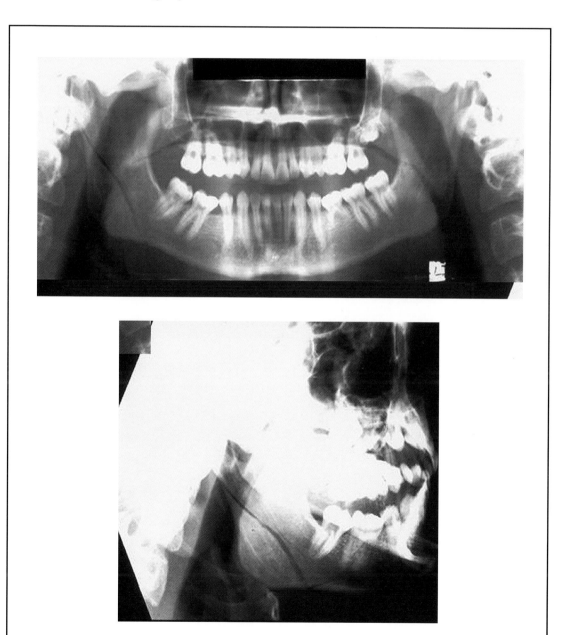

Answer to Case 84

There is a fracture of the right ramus and body, involving the lower aspect of the right condyle, demonstrated on both radiographs. The lucency of the left side is a composite shadow, not a fracture. Care is required when viewing OPG radiographs that composite shadows are not mistaken for fractures.

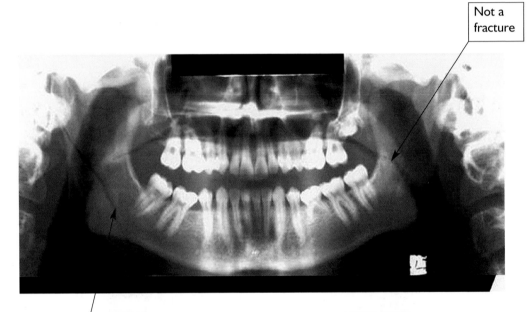

Not a fracture

Oblique fracture of right ramus and angle

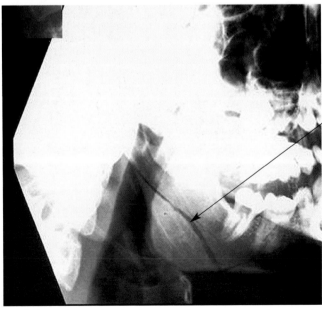

Oblique view demonstrating fracture of right ramus travelling forwards into body

Case 85

Patient fell on to mandible.

Describe the radiograph.

Are any further views required?

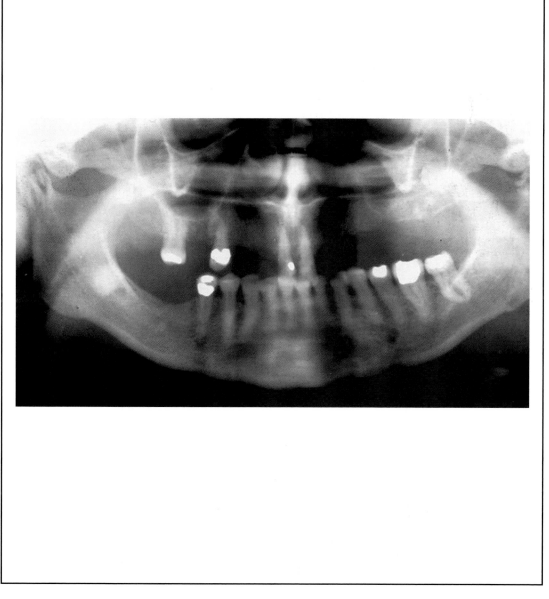

Answer to Case 85

There are probable fractures of both condyles. Also there is a subtle lucent line close to the left premolar. If this is clinically the area of injury then further intra-oral radiographs are required to rule out/confirm fracture. The intra-oral radiograph clearly demonstrates a fracture involving the tooth.

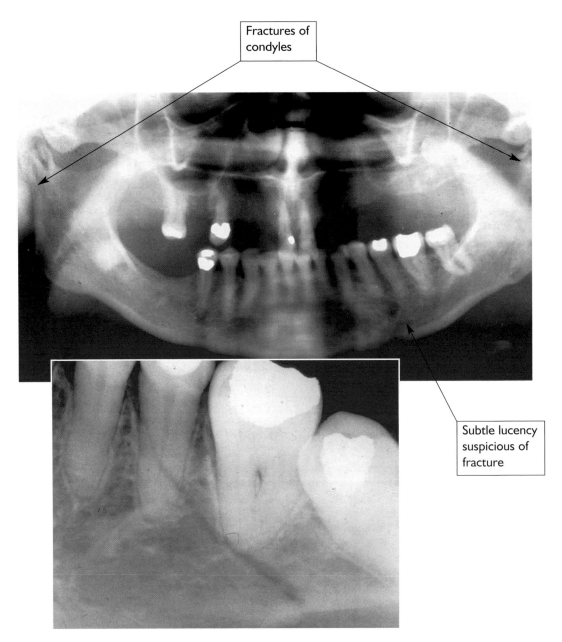

Fractures of condyles

Subtle lucency suspicious of fracture

Case 86

Child fell on to jaw while playing.

Describe the radiograph.

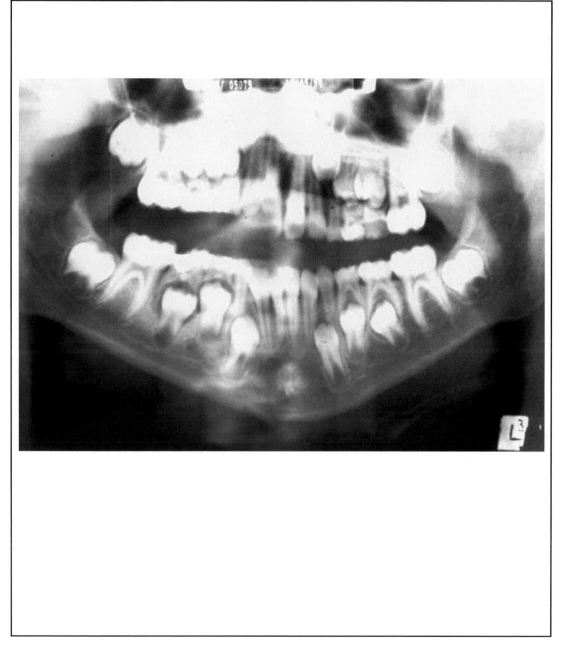

Answer to Case 86

There is a fracture of the symphysis – a difficult area to visualise in children and adults. Notice the second teeth in the alveolar area.

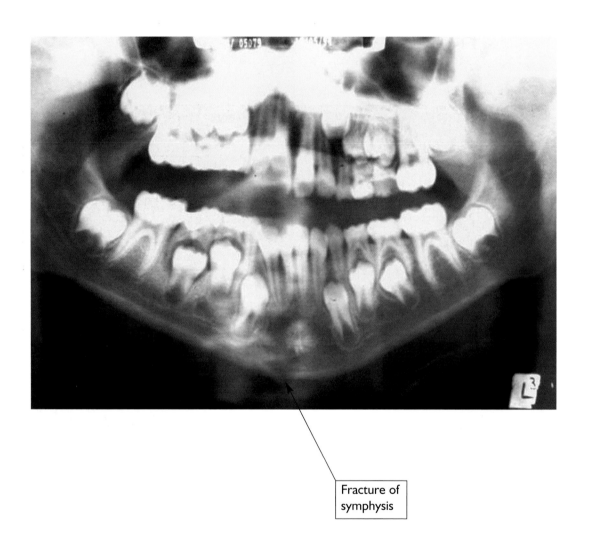

Fracture of symphysis

Case 87

Patient was involved in a fight.

Describe the radiograph.

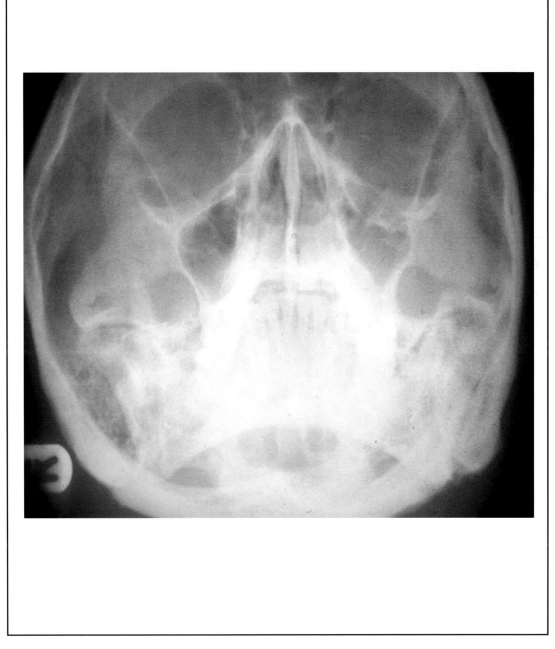

Answer to Case 87

There are fractures to the lateral border of the left maxillary sinus and the inferior border of the left eye.

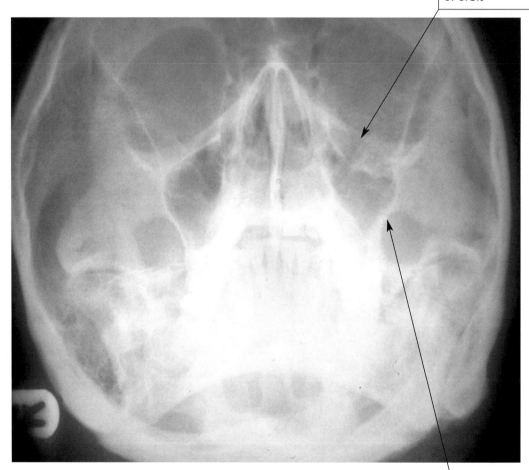

Fracture to inferior border of orbit

Fracture to lateral border of maxillary sinus

Case 88

Patient with facial trauma.

What is causing the overall unusual appearance on this radiograph?

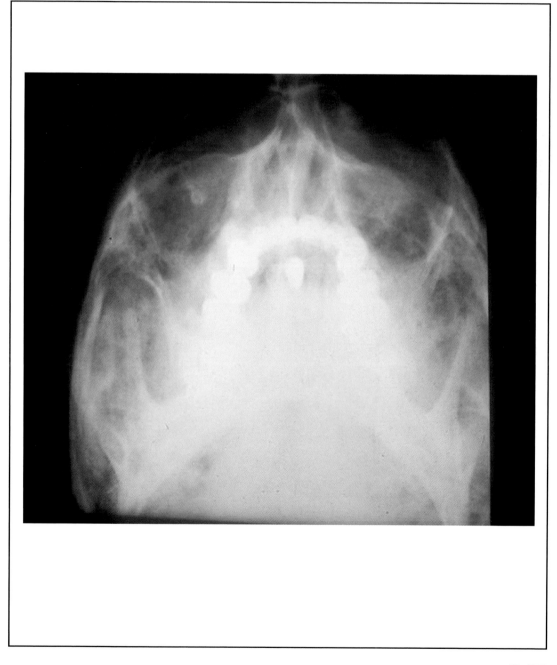

Answer to Case 88

The appearance is caused by air in the soft tissues which has escaped from the maxillary sinuses. This is emphysema; the lateral cervical spine demonstrates the air track downwards, towards the chest (demonstrated on the chest x-ray). This can sometimes result in a pneumo-mediastinum.

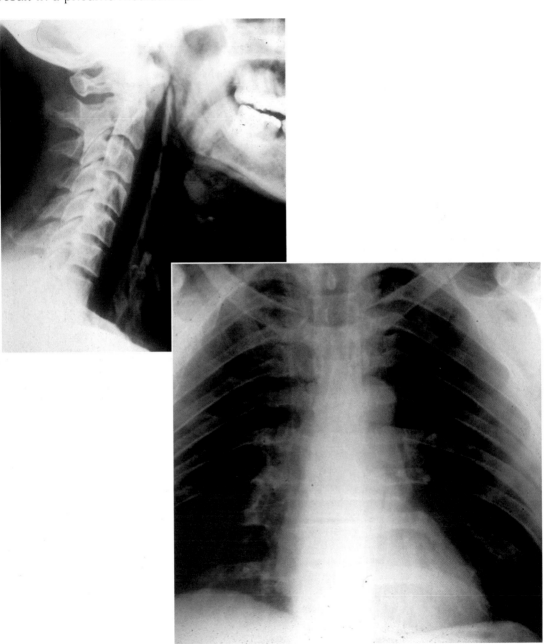

Case 89

Patient complained of continuing pain in both hips following a fall.

Describe the radiograph.

What is the cause of this appearance?

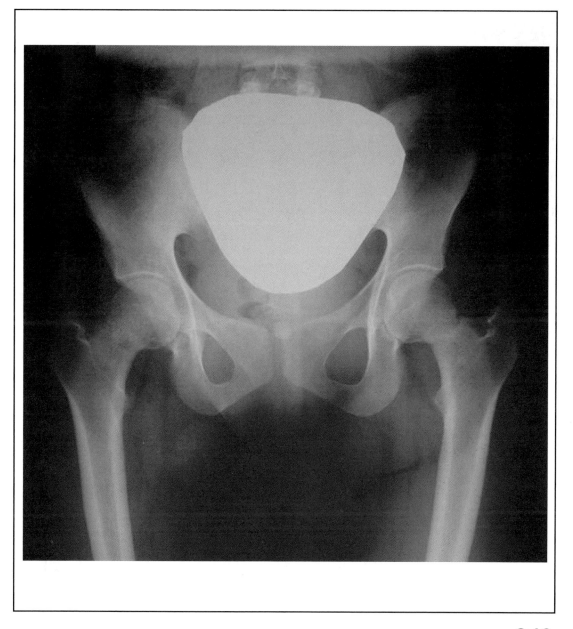

Answer to Case 89

There are bilateral transverse fractures of the femoral neck; these are called Looser's zones, and are caused by osteomalacia. Osteomalacia is an adult form of rickets due to a lack of mineralisation of normal osteoid, due to vitamin D deficiency. Common areas to find Looser's zones are femoral neck and lateral borders of scapulae (see pages 74–75).

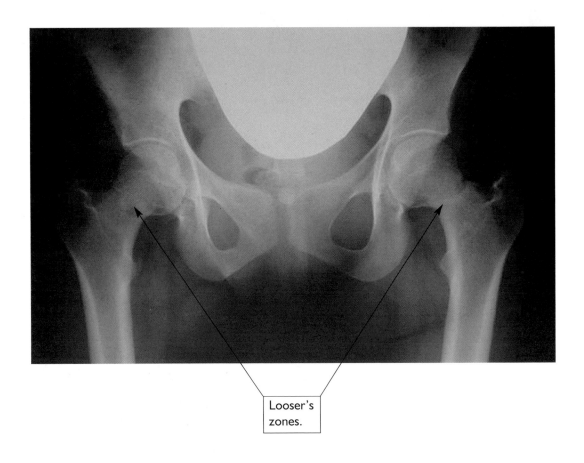

Looser's zones.

Case 90

Patient was involved in a road traffic accident.

Describe the radiographs.

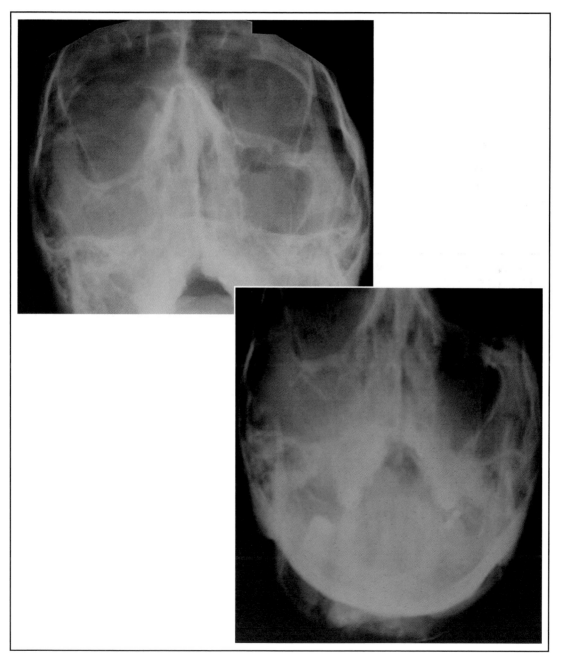

Answer to Case 90

The left maxillary antrum appears larger and more lucent than the right; it is filled with air (which appears black on radiographs). There also appears to be a fracture of the left inferior orbital border. With an open fracture of the maxillary antra, it is possible for air to enter and give this appearance.

Case 91

Patient was involved in a rugby tackle, injuring face.

Describe the radiograph.

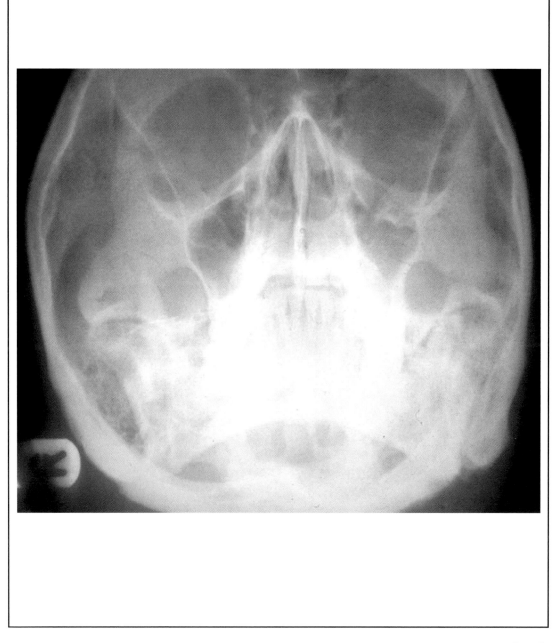

Answer to Case 91

There is a lucent line transversing the left inferior border of the orbit, indicative of a fracture. There is also probably a fracture of the lateral wall of the left maxillary antrum (identified by a lucent line). The CT scan confirms the fracture of the inferior orbital bone and demonstrates a fallen fragment of bone.

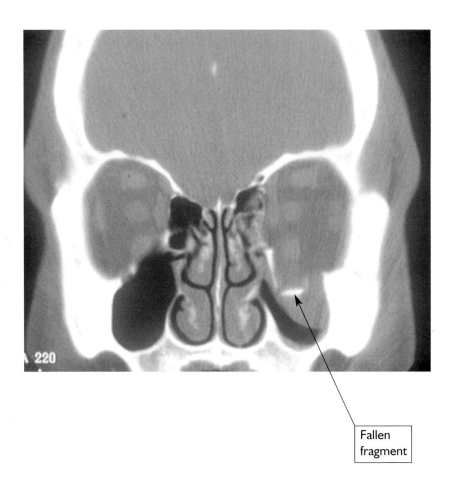

Fallen fragment

Case 92

Patient was involved in a road traffic accident.

Describe the radiograph

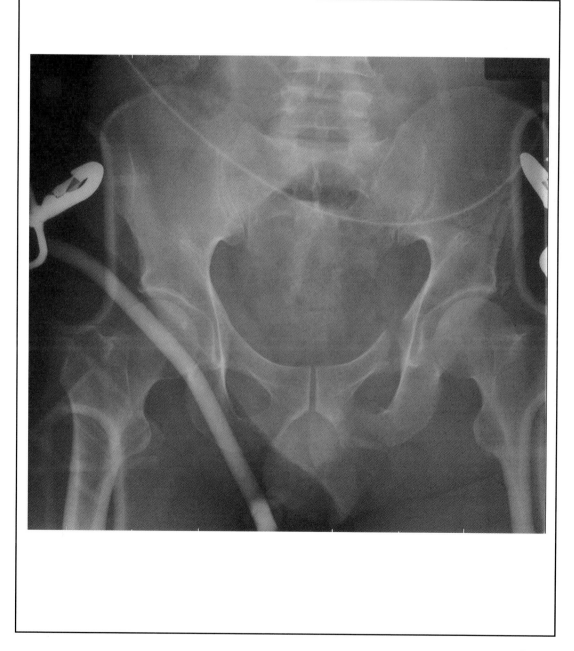

Answer to Case 92

There are clearly demonstrated fractures of the left superior and inferior pubic rami. This injury pattern would lead one to suspect an injury to the posterior pelvis, especially the sacral area. Remember the pelvis is like a bony ring. The sacrum is not clearly visualised on this radiograph, partially due to overlying bowel gas and being x-rayed on a spinal board. CT is required to ascertain any posterior pelvic injuries.

There is a suspicion of a fracture of the left ischium, but due to the spinal board this is difficult to confirm with any certainty.

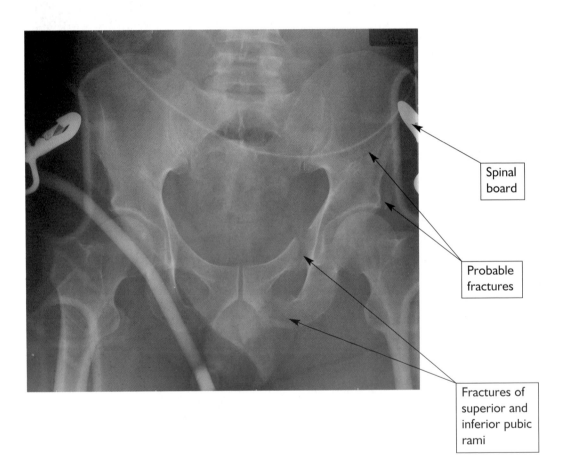

Spinal board

Probable fractures

Fractures of superior and inferior pubic rami

Case 93

Patient fell from a step while changing curtains. Patient has great difficulty weight bearing now, with pain in left hip.

Describe the radiographs.

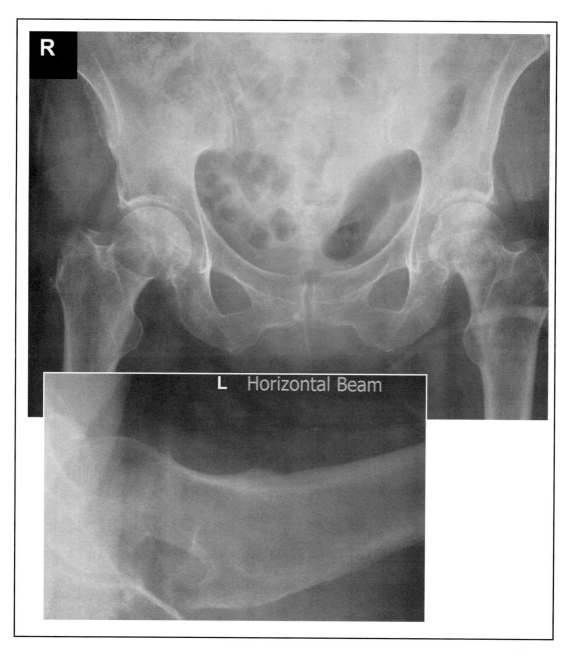

Answer to Case 93

There is a fracture of the left neck of femur, demonstrated on the antero-posterior radiograph by a step in the cortex and a sclerotic line; also the femoral neck now has a slightly valgus deformity. The lateral view confirms the diagnosis.

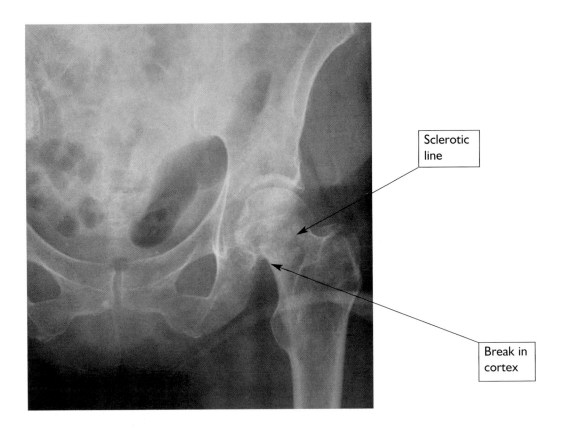

Sclerotic line

Break in cortex

Case 94

Patient hit a car and fell off bicycle. Describe the radiograph.

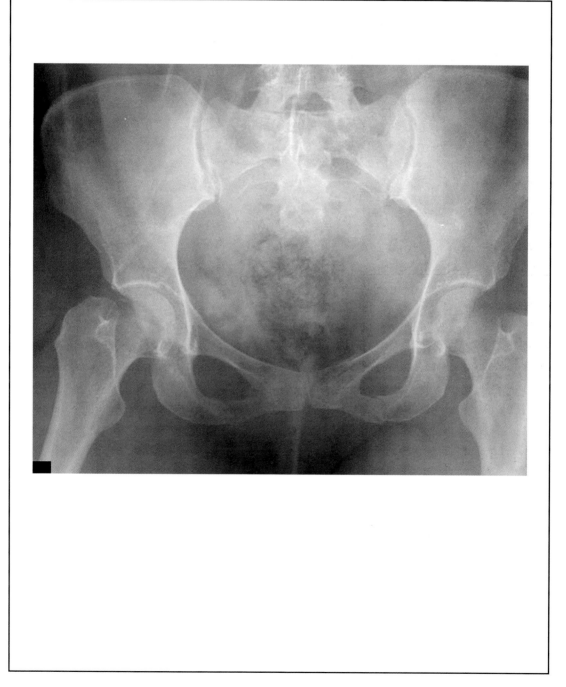

Answer to Case 94

There are fractures of the right and probably left inferior pubic rami. Remember when reviewing the trauma pelvis to treat it as a bony ring – if you see a fracture anteriorly then look for one posteriorly. There are fractures of the right sacral alar with slight widening of the right sacroiliac joint.

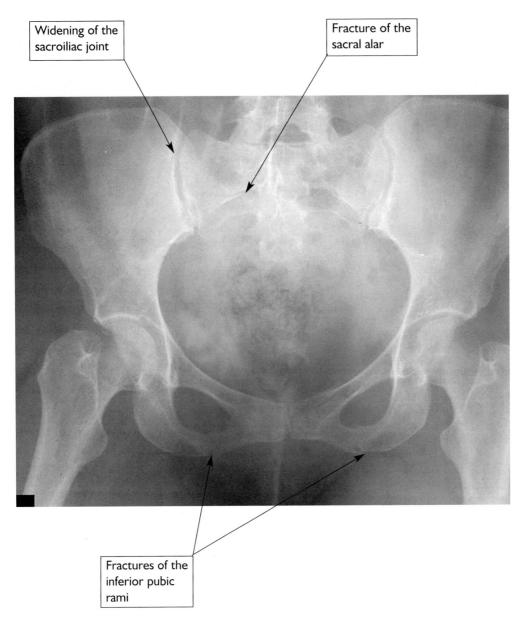

Widening of the sacroiliac joint

Fracture of the sacral alar

Fractures of the inferior pubic rami

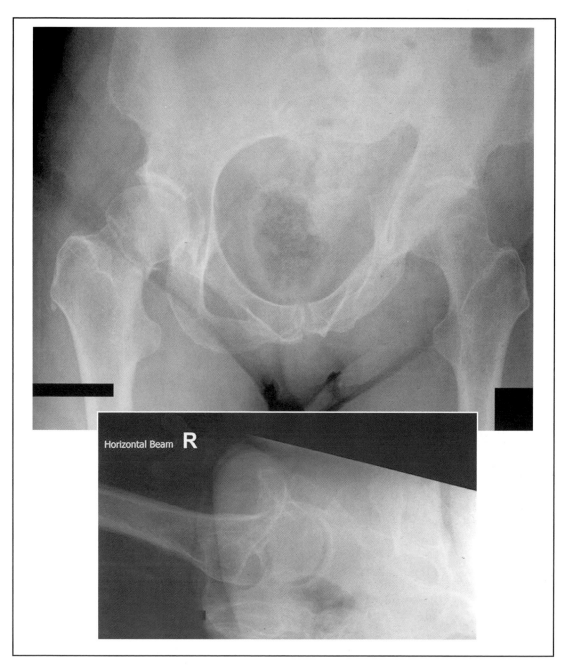

Case 95

Patient fell from wheelchair on to hip.

Describe the radiographs.

Horizontal Beam **R**

Answer to Case 95

There is a fracture of the right neck of the femur, near the lucent line caused by a soft tissue fold, on the anterior posterior radiograph. It is sometimes difficult to assess whether a fracture is present or not when it overlies a soft tissue fold, or when the anatomy is different from normal, as in this case. Often it is the second view that confirms whether or not there is a fracture.

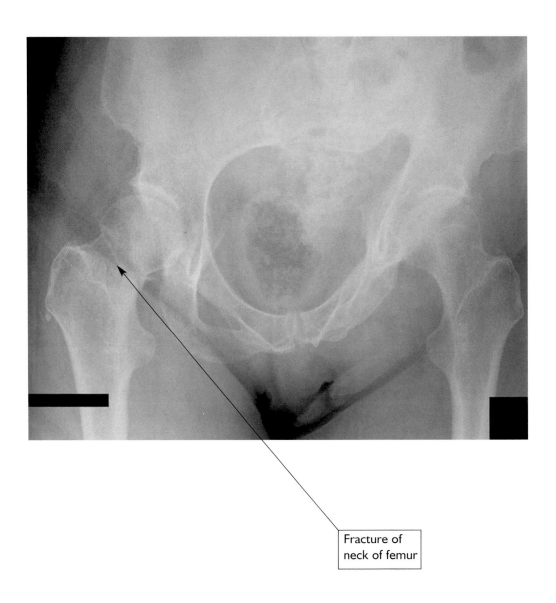

Fracture of
neck of femur

Case 96

Patient fell during athletic training, now has pain in right hip.

Before reviewing the Judet's views on the next page, can you see a reason why the clinician may have requested these radiographs?

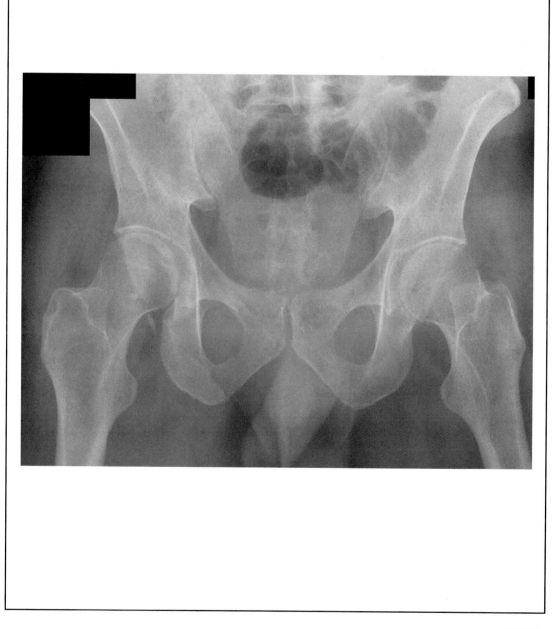

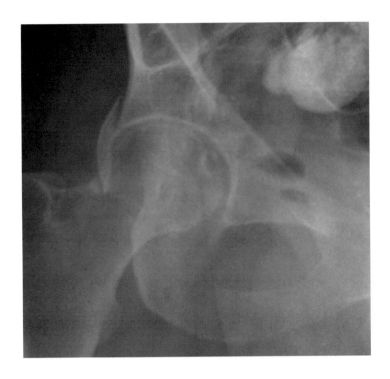

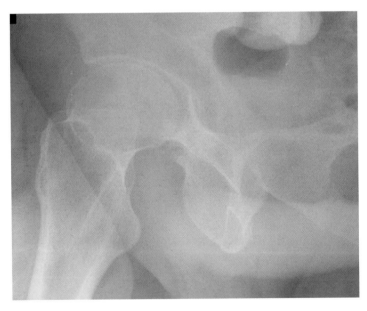

For answer see next page.

Answer to Case 96

The pelvis demonstrates an oblique lucent line in the right superior acetabulum. The bony fragment inferior to the hip appears well corticated, hence is not a new injury. One of the oblique views demonstrates an avulsion of the anterior superior iliac spine where the sartorius muscle attaches.

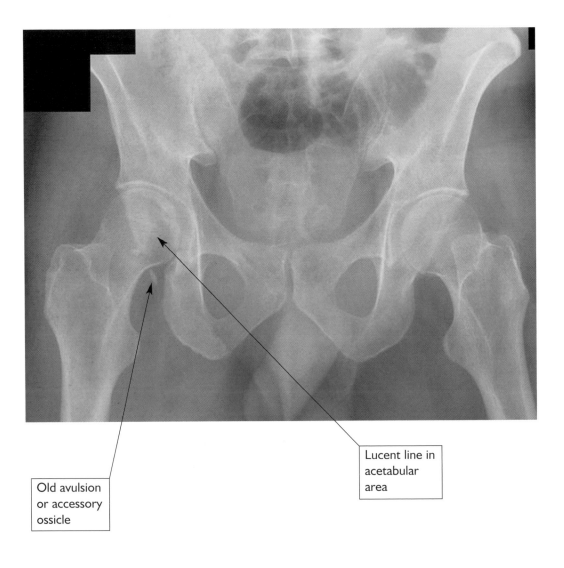

Lucent line in acetabular area

Old avulsion or accessory ossicle

Case 97

Patient was involved in a road traffic accident.

Describe the radiograph.

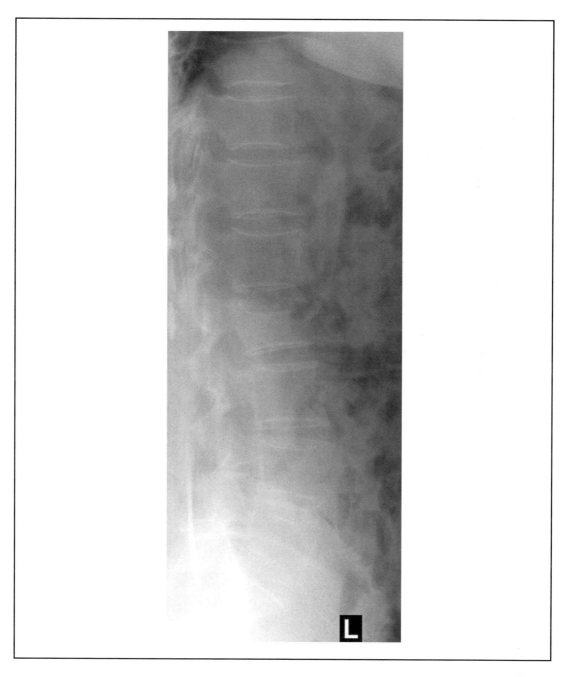

Answer to Case 97

There is a compressed wedge fracture of lumbar vertebra 2.

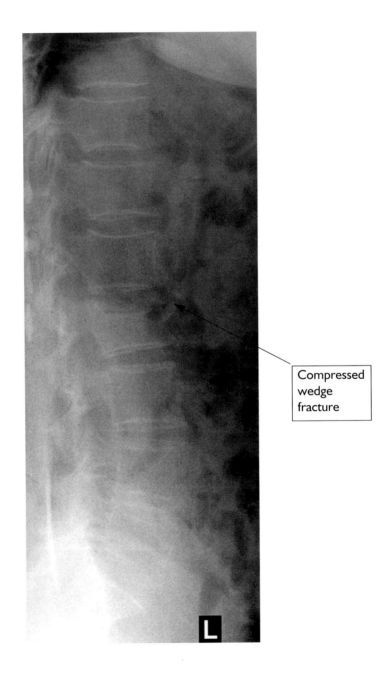

Compressed
wedge
fracture

Case 98

Patient was involved in a fight.

Describe the radiographs.

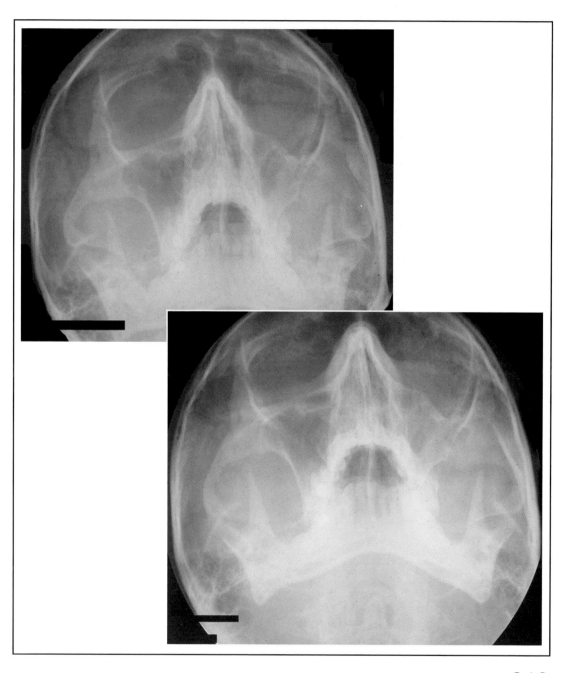

Answer to Case 98

There is a depressed fracture of the left orbital floor, with opacification of the left maxillary antrum, and a fracture through the left zygoma; with diastasis of fronto-zygomatic suture. There is a suspicion of a right zygomatic arch fracture.

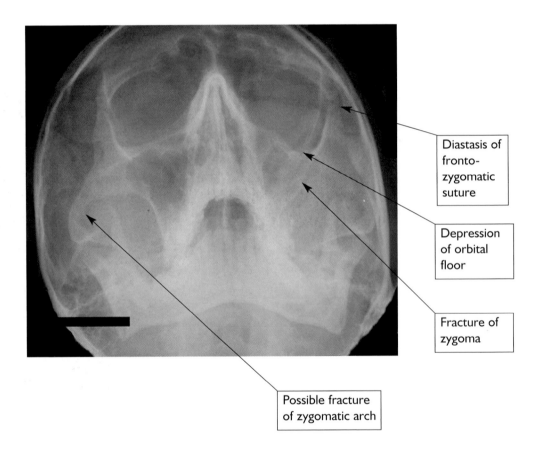

Diastasis of fronto-zygomatic suture

Depression of orbital floor

Fracture of zygoma

Possible fracture of zygomatic arch

Case 99

Patient was involved in a fight.

Describe the radiograph.

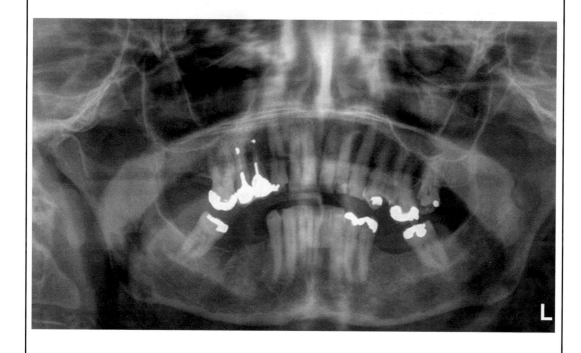

Answer to Case 99

There is an oblique fracture of the base of the left condyle.

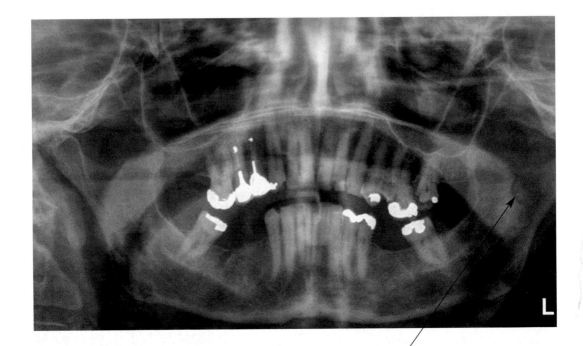

Oblique fracture
of condyle

Case 100

Patient fell from chair, now has pain in right hip.

Describe the radiographs

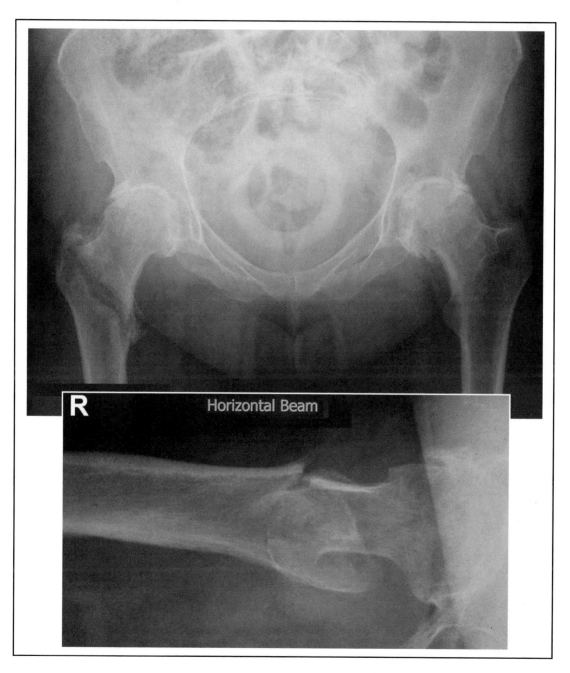

Answer to Case 100

There is an intertrochanteric fracture of the right hip.

Reading list and bibliography

Annals of the ICRP (1996). *Use of Ionising Radiation and its Application in Diagnostic Imaging.* London: ICRP.

Burnett, S., and Tyler, A. (2000). *A-Z of Orthopaedic Radiology.* London: W.B. Saunders.

Chapman, S., and Nakielny, R. (1995). *Aids to Radiological Differential Diagnosis*, 3rd edn. London: W.B. Saunders.

Dandy, D.J., and Edwards, D.J. (1998). *Essential Orthopaedics and Trauma*, 3rd edn. London: Churchill Livingstone.

Grainger, R.G., and Allison, D.J. (2001). *Diagnostic Radiology*, 4th edn. London: Churchill Livingstone.

Greenspan, A., and Gershwin, M.E. (1990). *Radiology of the Arthrides – a Clinical Approach.* London, NewYork: J.B. Lippincott, Gower Medical Publishing.

Helms, C.A. (1995). *Fundamentals of Skeletal Radiology*, 2nd edn. London: W.B. Saunders.

Keats, T. (2001). *Atlas of Normal Roentgen Variants that May Simulate Disease,* 7th edn. London: Mosby.

Manaster, B.J. (1989). *Handbooks in Radiology, Skeletal Radiology.* London: Year Book Medical Publishers.

National Institute for Clinical Excellence (NICE) (2003). *Head Injury. Triage, assessment, investigation and early management of head injury in infants, children and adults.* Clinical Guideline 4. London: NICE.

National Institute for Clinical Excellence (NICE) (2003, updated 2007). *Managing Head Injury.* London: NICE.

Nicholson, D.A., and Driscoll, P.A. (1995). *ABC of Emergency Radiology.* London: W.B. Saunders.

Raby, N., and de Lacey, G. (2005). *Accident and Emergency Radiology, a Survival Guide*, 2nd edn. London: Elsevier.

Renton, P. (1998). *Orthopaedic Radiology – Pattern Recognition and Differential Diagnosis*, 2nd edn. London: Martin Dunitz.

Rogers, L.F. (1992). *Radiology of Skeletal Trauma*, 2nd edn. London: Churchill Livingstone.

Royal College of Radiologists (2003). *Making the Best Use of a Department of Clinical Radiology*, 4th edn. London: RCR.

Sakthivel-Wainford, K. (2006). *Self Assessment in Limb X-ray Interpretation.* Keswick: M&K Update Ltd.

Sakthivel-Wainford, K. (2008). *Self Assessment in Paediatric Musculoskeletal Trauma X-rays.* Keswick: M&K Update Ltd.

Stoker, D.J., and Tilley, E.A. (1989). *Self Assessment in Radiology and Imaging 4 – Orthopaedics.* London: Wolfe

Medical Publications Ltd.

Sutton, D. (2002). *Textbook of Radiology and Imaging*, 7th edn. London: Elsevier.

Tile, M., and Pennel, G.F. (1980). 'Pelvic disruption: principles of management.' *Clinical Orthopaedics* 151: 56.

277